ANDREW JACKSON, HERO

Donald Barr Chidsey

ANDREW JACKSON, HERO

WILDSIDE PRESS

CONTENTS

To Frances

ANDREW JACKSON HERO

1

AN ASSAULT UPON THE WHITE HOUSE

They owned the world, these snorting, chortling, goggle-eyed visitors from the backwoods; or at least, they thought they did; they *felt* like that. It is certain that they owned Washington, into the streets of which, as into its environs, they had been pouring in packed, noisy columns for more than a week. Jubilant, whooping exuberantly, they had taken over the place. They had come to see and to cheer the Hero, the General, *their* President. Before the great day of March 4, 1829, they had been teeming into town—on horseback, in coaches and carriages, but most of them in wagons or drays. They slept wherever they could find room—on benches in taverns, on billiard tables, in the street.

"I never saw anything like it before," a certain congressman wrote to a friend in Massachusetts. "They really seem to think the country is rescued from some dreadful danger." Daniel Webster spoke in honest wonder, though wonder was not a habit of this man, who knew everything.

To another who was there, and who later was to become one of the Hero's most distinguished biographers, ". . . it seemed as if half the nation had rushed at once into the capital. It was like the inundation of the northern barbarians into Rome, save that the tumultuous tide came from a different point of the compass."

ANDREW JACKSON, HERO

Most of the newcomers in fact were from the West, a tousled lot, few of them in buckskin shirts, fewer still with raccoon tails on their hats, but rough, shaggy, and unattended by servants or slaves. It was their day. Until this time the chief magistrates had been men with slick manners, solemn and polished, glossy in their silks, their satin. Except for two Latin-quoting New Englanders they had all come from Virginia. Now, for the first time, there was to be a President of the United States from the other side of the mountains. Whoop-ee! The visitors crowded Pennsylvania Avenue to see him.

What they expected, no one knows. A hairy giant, perhaps, with a tomahawk in one hand, a hunting knife in the other? He had fought duels. He had whipped the Creeks and later the brassy British. He raced horses, he pitted cocks. Would he be beslobbered with blood? Would he grind his teeth, glaring as a tiger glares between the bars of its cage? Surely he did not fit into the Washington pattern.

As that same biographer was to remark, ". . . the ruling class in the United States, as in all other countries, was chiefly composed of men who had graduated at colleges, and had passed the great part of their lives on carpets," but this description certainly did not apply to Andrew Jackson. He was old, sixty-two, the oldest man ever to be elected President, and it was known that he carried within him a couple of ounce-and-a-half bullets. Would he limp? Would he grimace like an ape? What did he *look* like?

He had professed to admire the third President of the United States, the sage of Monticello, but Thomas Jefferson was known to have expressed dismay when he heard that Andrew Jackson was being mentioned as a presidential possibility. "He is one of the most unfit men I know of for the place . . . he is a dangerous man." However, there was one thing these two had in common. They both hated to speak in public, and when duty compelled them to do so they mumbled, chin down, so that nobody beyond the second row could hear.

Only one political party existed in the United States, yet in the "campaign" just finished there had been a most extraordinary burst of name-calling, scheming, manoeuvering for high position. What speechifying there had been, stump and platform, was done by minor personages, not the candidates themselves, who would have lowered themselves by a public display of their persons. This man Jackson had done all of his fighting—and a prodigious amount of it there must have been!—on the other side of the Alleghenies. He might as well have done it in Outer Mongolia. True, he had served in the United States Senate for a short while, in the House of Representatives briefly before that, but that had been many years ago, and he had not made much of an impression upon the professionals. Those who remembered him at all did so dimly, picturing a lank person whose hair, red, long, and exceedingly straight, had been clubbed into an old eelskin. This did little to help those who had surged out of the wilderness.

Andrew Jackson had been in the capital for several weeks, having entered it quietly and without escort after a quiet trip from his home near Nashville, Tennessee, but he had remained in seclusion upstairs at the Indian Queen, the best inn in town, popularly known as the Wigwam, and few had even glimpsed him at a window. Washington barbers were offering Jackson haircuts, just as Washington haberdashers were advertising Jackson stocks, but nobody really *knew*.

The upper half of Pennsylvania Avenue was paved, though the lower half, down near the Executive Mansion, like all other thoroughfares in this raw new city remained in its primitive state of mud or dust, depending upon the season. Now, on Inauguration Day, the President-elect would march up this street to the Capitol, where he would take the oath of office.

With necks craned and strained, eyes popping like Ping-Pong balls, the people waited. They were not a mob. They were orderly, expectant, even joyful.

At last he came.

13

He was tall and unexpectedly thin. You could have wound your hands around his chest, you thought. He wore no uniform—many of those in the crowd must have expected enormous flapping epaulettes, at least—and he carried no sword, but his mien was invincibly military. He stood erect, head back. The famous hair was no longer red, but rather a hesitant gray moving toward unrelieved whiteness, and there was plenty of it. The chin was a pump handle. The eyes were azure, and they said damn you. Here was a man.

He was hatless, an extraordinary condition in a day when a man, any man, would no more think of going outdoors without a hat than he would think of going out without trousers. The men around Andrew Jackson, a sort of honor guard of office seekers, were properly hatted, as they were mounted, but the President-elect elected to walk.

He looked up at Capitol Hill, and his stare was stony. How dare that eminence get in his way! He started for it.

The political campaign just closed had been the dirtiest in the history of the United States. Among the charges made by one newspaper that opposed Jackson was that his wife Rachel smoked a corncob pipe (which was true) and that she had once been a whore (which was not). Before the candidate could answer this effrontery as he would have wished—that is, with a horsewhip—the lady in question, a gentle, motherly soul, died. Jackson had just been elected, but his beloved Rachel was not to go with him to Washington, where he would take the oath of office. Instead, they buried her in the garden of their home, the Hermitage.

"Tuberculosis," the doctor had said. But Jackson knew better; he avowed that his wife "was murdered by slanders that pierced her heart." He blamed John Quincy Adams, the President he was to succeed, for the whole business, something Adams, a waspish man, vehemently denied.

14

AN ASSAULT UPON THE WHITE HOUSE

Although the President-elect had stayed at the Wigwam in Washington for two weeks before the inauguration, he had not called at the Executive Mansion. This was considered a serious breach of etiquette, but etiquette was the last thing in the world Andrew Jackson worried about. On March 2 the President wrote to the President-elect to tell him that the house was his any time. He himself, Adams reported, was moving to Commodore David Porter's old house on Meridian Hill in the western part of Washington. Jackson replied with a cold, formal thank-you note, nothing more. Adams did not go to the inauguration.

The custom of giving U.S. Army leaders unflattering yet affectionate nicknames had not yet been instituted. Old Fuss and Feathers, Old Rough and Ready, Old Ironpants, Old Blood and Guts—these were in the future. Andrew Jackson must have been the first. Admiring soldiers out west, far from any newspaper, had dubbed him—spontaneously, it would seem, because of his terrible tenacity, his durability—Old Hickory. The rest of the world approved. The crowd along Pennsylvania Avenue undoubtedly knew about the bullets the General carried, and some of them might have heard that there were times when this old man could hardly walk and that few days passed in which he did not suffer from coughing hemorrhages and from chills and fever. This knowledge only touched up the tales of his steely will.

It could be that there was, lurking in that crowd, his mouth an O, the same boy who a few years later was to be asked by his Sunday school teacher about the immortality potential of President Jackson. "Now, when *he* dies will *he* go to Heaven, too?" The boy hesitated only for a moment. "He will if he wants to," was the reply.

The President-elect mounted the hill with swinging strides. Some of the horsemen had trouble keeping up with him. The scene at the Capitol itself—Jackson would be the first to take the oath out-of-doors—is best described by Margaret Bayard Smith, a noted hostess, who was no name-dropper, and who was assuredly not a person to be awed by the presence of fame:

Thousands and thousands of people, without distinction of rank, collected in an immense mass round the Capitol, silent, orderly and tranquil, with their eyes fixed on the front of that edifice, waiting the appearance of the President in the portico. The door from the Rotunda opens, preceded by the marshals, surrounded by the Judges of the Supreme Court, the old man with his grey locks, that crown of glory, advances, bows to the people, who greet him with a shout that rends the air. The Cannons, from the heights around, from Alexandria and Fort Warburton proclaim the oath he has taken and all the hills reverberate the sound. It was grand,—it was sublime! An almost breathless silence succeeded and the multitude was still,—listening to catch the sound of his voice, tho' it was so low, as to be heard only by those nearest to him.

It was after that that the assault upon the Executive Mansion occurred.

The new President belonged to the people, didn't he? Then should not his house be the people's house? After the Hero had mumbled his inaugural speech, after the ceremony was finished, he put on a hat and mounted a horse and rode down the hill, presumably headed for 1600 Pennsylvania Avenue, his official residence, and the crowd, always friendly, thought it would be a right neighborly plan to pay him a visit. Halloing, they too went down the hill. There was to be some kind of reception in the Executive Mansion, they had heard. Good. They enveloped the place. They inundated it.

No defense was possible. No gate guarded the building known to most men as the Executive Mansion or the President's Residence, though a few, in Washington itself, were beginning to call it the White House. No wall had been built around it; no guards had been appointed for its protection. The crowd simply swept up the carriage drive, or across the lawn, and plunged in.

The captain was not aboard, and the regular staff of servants, sixteen in number, had no one to appeal to. The cheering thousands, the great unwashed, took over.

It was not comparable to the Paris mob crashing into the Petit Trianon, or the Gordon rioters stoning M.P.'s as they emerged from their hall, or anything like that. This was a good-natured horde. They trampled the rugs with their dusty boots, but did not rip them to pieces. They broke a few windows, but not in anger, only by accident because the push was so great. True, men stood on chairs, which was not good for the expensive stuff with which the chairs were covered, but they did this only because they wanted to see over the heads of their fellow visitors; they did not *smash* those chairs. True, here and there a scuffling sort of fight might have broken out, a nose or a mouth been bloodied, but that was not the rule, and anyway for the most part there simply wasn't room to swing a fist. Glasses were shattered, inevitably, but the only things that the citizens stole were, as might have been expected, some spoons, souvenirs. The house was not looted. This was a friendly, folksy visit.

Most of the men in the churning mass, even those among them who could be rated as gentlemen, chewed tobacco, and so they spat. Oh, how they spat! The "palace" at that time was not equipped with cuspidors, and the callers expectorated upon the carpet, upon the satin-covered chairs, upon the lovely damask draperies, and often, such was their closeness, upon one another. The air reeked of shag spittle.

Cakes, ice cream, and orange punch had been placed on long tables in the otherwise skimpily furnished East Room, and these were eaten, drunk, or spilled. Clod-hoppered callers took to swooping upon the laden servants as soon as they emerged from the kitchens, and that compounded the confusion. Even after somebody had the idea of carrying the comestibles out

17

on the lawn in tubs, thus luring away some of the visitors, the chaos in the East Room continued, the noise was not abated.

Unnoticed in the midst of all this, for all his height, blinking in bewilderment, a stranger in his own house, stood Andrew Jackson.

After the inauguration the Hero had returned to the Indian Queen to lie down for a while. Then he had made his way to 1600 Pennsylvania Avenue, to see how the reception was going.

He had ordered that refreshments be set out, true, and that the place be thrown open to the public, but he had never expected anything like this. He was appalled.

The wonder was that Jackson wasn't crushed to death. This spindly President was a spectre, a death's-head, and when he was caught up in the swirl of humanity and slammed against a wall by men who would have hoisted him on their shoulders if they had known who he was, he could scarcely keep his feet. Jackson had arrived in the company of two friends, Representative and Mrs. John Floyd. After failing to get the attention of any of the servants, the Floyds, together with their two stout sons, formed a bodyguard for the Chief Magistrate, and ran interference for him in a wedge, hustling him unharmed to a side door and so back to the Wigwam, where he lay down again.

Not until the next afternoon, when most of the debris had been broomed off and many of the rips in the upholstery sewn, did he venture again to the White House.

Nevertheless, those revelers, every last stomping, shouting, spitting one of them, were right. The country *had* been "rescued from some dreadful danger," and Andrew Jackson *was* their President. Things would never be the same again.

2

THE FIERCEST MAN

What manner of man was Jackson? How did he get that way? Upon what meat, in other words, was this our particular Caesar fed?

He was of Gaelic extraction, and oppugnancy was built into him. His parents, poor but not penniless, had come to the New World from Carrickfergus, Ireland, in 1765. They had two sons then. They landed at Charleston, South Carolina, and went upcountry to buy a small plantation on the banks of the Twelve Mile Creek. This was in a settlement called Waxhaws, though whether it was located in Union County, North Carolina, or Lancaster County, South Carolina, is a matter that historians to this day have not decided. (The governors of the two states met at Waxhaws some years after Jackson's time to decide upon the line, a conference that was memorable chiefly because of the Governor of North Carolina's remark to the Governor of South Carolina that it was a damn long time between drinks; but the Jackson homestead no longer existed then, and its site could not be ascertained.)

It was at Waxhaws, a little more than a year and a half after he had reached the land of promise, that the immigrant died, possibly of overwork; he had never been a strong man. A few days after that the third son was born, an orphan from the start, and was christened Andrew, Jr. His mother moved in with her married sister, who lived not far away.

Young Andrew, a gangling redhead, was eight years old when Major Pitcairn's men came swinging into the murky pre-dawn at Lexington to start a conflict that was to last for nine weary years. In the South this was war at its worst, a war of split families and house burnings, of small but exceedingly ferocious fights between neighbors, followed, often, by the hanging of those who had lost. It was, in short, civil war, and when, toward its end, the redcoats came in splendid array, they were looked upon only as meddlesome outsiders, intruders.

Andrew Jackson was in it, be sure of that! Though he was only a boy, and going to school from time to time, he joined the Patriot forces, irregular forces, along with his two brothers. If he could not tote a musket, if he did not know what to do on a parade ground, at least he had long legs, so he could be useful as a runner, a messenger. It is certain that he was present at Hanging Rock, one of the fracases big enough to rate a name. It is certain, too, that he survived.

His brothers did not. One was killed in action, obscurely. The other died in jail, a prisoner of war. Andrew himself spent at least a little while in prison. In addition, his mother, who had been working among Patriot prisoners afflicted with small-pox in a British jail in Charleston, herself caught the disease and died of it.

Andrew was left utterly alone, but that did not faze him. He served as an apprentice to a harness maker, and he studied law both in Charleston and in Salisbury, North Carolina, where, still in his teens, he was admitted to the bar. He even taught school for a little while.

Unexpectedly, a relative died in the Old Country and left Jackson £ 300. He went to Charleston and bought some fine clothes, attended cockfights and horse races, and patronized brothels. He learned how to play brag, a card game out of which poker was to grow, and hazard, a dice game, yawning when he lost. In short, he became a gentleman.

When the money was gone he did what many another young

man of the time was doing in the absence of financial expectations or of family influence: he went west.

West, the other side of the mountains, was the wild frontier. To Andrew Jackson it meant the western district of North Carolina, the land that some called by its Indian name of Tennessee.

There is a tradition in Jonesboro that Andrew Jackson came into that town just west of the Appalachians one bright spring morning, and he was riding one horse and leading another, upon which a mulatto girl sat perched while a pack of foxhounds followed him. This is to be doubted. Fox hunting—"the unspeakable in pursuit of the inedible," Oscar Wilde was to call it—was unknown in the western district of North Carolina. He could only have acquired a pack of hounds by making an expensive side trip into Virginia, and if he had had that much money left he would almost undoubtedly have spent it on a third horse or a second girl rather than on dogs.

No matter. However equipped, Jackson fitted into the life of the West. There was always work for a lawyer in any land occupied by white Americans, the most disputatious persons in the world, who were always suing or countersuing one another.

Friends later in life were fond of pointing to Andrew Jackson's job record as a bright example of the great United States rags-to-riches tradition—a lawyer at nineteen, United States attorney at twenty-three, congressman at twenty-nine, United States senator at thirty, and justice of the Supreme Court of Tennessee at thirty-one—but in fact there was nothing especially notable about it, given the circumstances. He held none of these positions very long, and he didn't like any of them, except the justiceship. Of course he had many clients; of course he was a delegate to the constitutional convention that was to make Tennessee a state; and of course he was one of that state's first congressmen—that much could be taken for granted. He certainly had no sensation of climbing a ladder.

"Success" then, as now, meant making money, and for

most of Andrew Jackson's nonmilitary life in Tennessee he was not making money but was, rather, in debt. There was very little cash in that part of the world—the Eastern bankers kept it on their side of the mountains, men said—and clients often paid in kind. Jackson accepted, perforce, whiskey, cotton, hemp, slaves—but most of all, land. Land was everything. Men bought it and sold it, dickered for it, and connived to control it, in great batches, in princely parcels. Five thousand acres was a mere side yard for any Tennessee speculator, who might not be able to buy his wife a second dress. The federal government, otherwise indigent at the end of the Revolution, paid its veterans largely in lands that lay on the sunset side of the mountains, and the veterans, needing something more readily negotiable, sold the deeds to this countryside they never had seen to Eastern bankers and speculators, who likewise never had seen it. Ownership gradually moved west, where it belonged, and penniless Tennesseans went into a perfect frenzy of gambling, tossing uncounted acres upon the table, losing them, winning them, mortgaging them, exchanging them.

True, from time to time even the biggest operators had to turn aside for the purpose of picking up a living. Thus, Andrew Jackson had his law business. He also indulged in the building of riverboats on order, and with a partner he opened a general store and trading post near Nashville. He had to sell out his half interest in this store when circumstances over which he had no control virtually forced him into bankruptcy, and at the same time too, and for the same reason, he was obliged to put aside his plans for the building of a plantation house to be called the Hermitage. But he never stopped dealing in land, and never stopped believing that fame and fortune lay in the next valley, just over that hilly horizon.

And of course he always found time to fight.

He had entered Tennessee—with or without the foxhounds or the doxy of Senegambian antecedents—in the spring of 1788.

That same year he fought his first duel. It was with a man named Waitsill Avery, another lawyer. We don't know what it was about, and perhaps they were not too clear on this point themselves.

Pistols on the frontier were of three sorts. There was the huge holster pistol or horse pistol, a heavy piece of mechanism. There was the derringer—sometimes spelled with only one *r*, the way its inventor, Henry, did—which was tiny and meant to be kept under an armpit or even up a sleeve. The derringer had a very large caliber, and fired an enormous ball. It would not carry far, but it was deadly at close quarters. It was primarily a scare weapon, favored by gamblers. The third kind was the dueling pistol. These always came in pairs, and were contained in handsome boxes lined with velvet on which were also mounted tweezers, lead molds, sometimes scales, always powder flasks and measuring scoops. The pistols themselves often were chased and damascened, or inlaid with gold, silver, ivory. Still, like the derringers and the horse pistols, they were smooth-bored, unreliable, touchy.

It is not known what weapons Jackson and Avery used, but Avery, much the older man, was probably like Jackson himself a poor shot. Anyway, they both missed.

At this time, Jackson also had horrific run-ins with two other lawyers of whose courtroom conduct he disapproved, but these arguments never reached the trigger-pulling stage, being blocked by friends. The men were John McNairy and William Cocke.

With General John ("Nolichucky Jack") Sevier it was different. He was a man of arms, a Revolutionary hero, one of the leaders at King's Mountain. Additionally, he was one of the most popular figures in the western district of North Carolina and had been governor of the new state, called Franklin at first, soon afterward Tennessee. "Nolichucky Jack," a famous fighter, was the father of eighteen children—some of them legitimate—which in itself would have made him a hero on the frontier.

While stump-speaking in a Tennessee city, this paragon spotted Andrew Jackson crossing the square near at hand, and in a loud voice he called to question the validity of Jackson's marriage to the former Rachel Donelson. Sevier got the action he must have sought. Jackson was carrying a cane, and he waved it as he charged through the crowd. "Good God, you dare to mention *her* sacred name!" Bystanders brought him down, and literally carried him back to his hotel, where, fuming, he wrote a challenge.

The two men never did actually meet on the field of honor, although several times arrangements were made for such a meeting, and at least once they faced one another with drawn pistols at a preselected place. Nevertheless, the public considered it a done duel, and Andrew Jackson, not until then a notably popular figure, was much applauded for his spunk in taking on the paladin.

The Donelsons were not rich, but they were many. They had cousins all over that part of the country. Jackson had met Rachel when as a young lawyer he patronized the Nashville boardinghouse run by her sister and where Rachel lived with her husband, Lewis Robards. She could hardly have been beautiful even then, and it was obvious to all that she and her husband were not getting along together. Jackson fell in love. He was to remain that way for the rest of his life.

It is hardly likely that Jackson and Rachel had an affair, but rumor of course created one. When Robards at last disappeared and they heard that he had obtained a divorce in Virginia, they got married right away. More than two years passed before they learned that only then had Robards at last got a divorce. The previous action had been no more than a grant of permission on the part of the Virginia legislature to *seek* a divorce. Jackson as a lawyer might have been expected to know the difference between a grant of permission and an actual bill of divorcement, but he hadn't. The Jacksons promptly remarried, to make everything legal, but for some time there they had been technically living in sin, and that was something Jackson's enemies did not allow him to forget.

Jackson's duties and his business deals often took him away from home, but his heart was always there. The Hermitage, after a couple of false starts, grew and grew, but it was never, then, a showplace; it was, however, where Rachel was.

The lady of the Hermitage was by some standards no lady at all. She wasn't *literally* illiterate. She could write her name and several other words as well. She did smoke a pipe, but she did not spit in public, and her manners were mild, if not elegant, her voice low. Children loved her. Everybody who knew her loved Rachel, a gentle woman, a good woman, deeply religious, the perfect homebody. She and Andrew—though there were several miscarriages—never had any children of their own, but they adopted no fewer than eleven boys from time to time, most of them nephews or cousins of Rachel, others orphans, one an Indian.

Jackson's Truxtun, a stallion, was the best money-maker in his stable. He matched it against Colonel Ervin's Plowboy, the purse to be $5,000, each owner to pay $700 if he defaulted. Ervin did default, and paid. But Ervin's son-in-law, a beefy lad named Dickinson, was overheard by somebody to say that Jackson had been heard complaining that the notes that made up the forfeit were not the ones agreed upon. (There were no federal bank notes in that part of the country then, only state and private bank notes, which varied widely in value.)

Jackson had had words with this young man before. It had been reported to him that Dickinson had made some slurring remark about the former Rachel Donelson, and Jackson had demanded an apology. Dickinson had replied that he did not remember saying such a thing, but if he had done so it must have been when he was drunk, and he was sorry.

Now Jackson went to Colonel Ervin, who promised to reprimand his son-in-law. Ervin also published a statement attesting to the proper form of the forfeit payment. That should have ended it. But Andrew Jackson, a he-man among he-men if ever there was one, was curiously womanlike in one respect: he took everything personally; to him nothing was abstract. Now he began to believe that this whole business was a plot to entice him into the field, for Charles Dickinson not only was a crack rifle shot, he was also a "natural" with a pistol, a man who never missed, who shot from the hip.

Jackson may have been right, but if so he went about it in the wrong way. He wrote to Dickinson again, demanding another apology, and this time the young man snarled back. The two began calling one another names, as was the custom of the time. By means of a series of letters in local newspapers, each announced to the world that the other was a coward, a poltroon, a hypocrite, a liar, and a generally unreliable citizen. Not until Dickinson ventured upon the use of "adulterer," however, did Superior Court Judge Jackson challenge him. Dickinson instantly accepted, naming Dr. Hanson Catlett as his representative. Jackson named General Thomas Overton.

That was May 22, 1806. The duel was set for the thirtieth on the Kentucky bank of the Red River just over the Tennessee line, a good day's ride due north of Nashville. The distance was to be eight paces instead of the usual ten.

Jackson and his friend went alone, thoughtful. Dickinson made a party of it, with gay companions. They stopped at an ordinary for drinks, and Dickinson, in high good spirits, demonstrated his skill with a pistol by cutting a string stretched between two twigs twenty-four feet away. He did not squint along the barrel of the gun. He did not aim. And he laughed all the while.

On the field the distance, murderously short, was paced

off. It was chilly, and neither principal shed his coat. Jackson's coat was a long, loose, capelike one, buttoned clear up to the chin.

Loaded pistols that were not cocked were placed in the men's hands. Their arms were at their sides, the muzzles of the guns down. They did not face one another but rather faced General Overton, who had won the toss to give the signal, and who stood halfway between them but well off to one side. They were told that General Overton would speak the one word, "Fire," and that then they should turn toward one another and shoot. They were asked separately if they were ready, and each replied that he was.

"*Fire!*"

Young Dickinson got his shot off instantly. Jackson, even after that explosion, continued to raise his right arm.

"Great God! Have I missed him?"

Dickinson instinctively stepped back, amazed. General Overton commanded him to resume his stand.

In fact, Dickinson had not missed. His bullet had gone right to the place where Jackson's heart would have been had not Jackson, in turning, twisted his body to the right under that long concealing cloak. (He was, remember, an extremely skinny man.) The bullet had penetrated the cloak, chipped the breastbone and two ribs, and skittered around *under the skin* to a place perilously near the heart, where it stopped. Jackson was bleeding like a pig. He must have been in terrible pain, but he didn't flinch.

While the others watched, fascinated, Dickinson white with fear, Jackson raised his pistol until he could sight. He squeezed the trigger. There was no explosion. The striker had fallen only to half cock, where it was caught.

Under the agreed-upon rules this did not constitute a shot, and Jackson was so informed. He knew it anyway. With his thumb, not otherwise moving, he recocked the weapon. Charles

27

Dickinson simply stood there, waiting to be murdered.

Jackson shot him through the stomach, and he went down.

Overton took his principal's pistol and led him from the firing line. Then, as custom required, he went to the group around Dickinson, bowed, and asked if he might be of any further service. He was assured that there was nothing he could do. He bowed again and left the field arm-in-arm with Andrew Jackson, who never wavered, though by this time the blood had run clear down his body and was filling his left boot. They could hear Charles Dickinson screaming in pain behind them. Out of sight of Dickinson's friends, Jackson collapsed.

"I would have hit him," he said later, "if he had shot me through the brain."

Dickinson died at nine o'clock that night. Jackson was in bed for a month.

3

CALL TO ARMS

He was edging middle age, a rigid man with a mouth like a mail slot, and he knew that there were things to do more important than slaying slanderous whippersnappers. For he was in the army now. Properly, he was in the Tennessee militia.

This was natural. Every man in those parts was expected to serve at least one term in the militia. However, Jackson, whose previous military experience had been that of a camp follower, a boy, was, in Tennessee, one of the top brass, the commander in chief.

He had not come up through the ranks. In 1792 he had been appointed judge advocate of the militia in Davidson County. This position carried with it the rank and title of colonel, but it was purely political, not military at all. Ten years later he went after the big prize, the commandership. This too was a political appointment, and an important one, for the head of the militia in Tennessee was generally rated as the second man in the state. It was particularly desirable in Andrew Jackson's eyes in that year of 1802 because his principal opponent in the council of militia staff officers who named the commander in chief was a follower of Jackson's pet enemy, John Sevier, who sought by this means to consolidate his position as the top political boss.

Jackson won—by one vote! Thereafter, in part because of

the prestige of the title, his fortunes bettered. Through all these years, since the failure of a friend in Philadelphia had embarrassed him, Andrew Jackson had been a serious, conservative, hard-working man of business. But business, like his horses (Truxtun excepted), had not paid him well. Now, however, things began to pick up. He was able to take better care of Rachel, and he started to build the real Hermitage, the one he had dreamed of.

His health was worse than ever, but that did not prevent him from taking the field at the head of his troops when the nation went to war in 1812. They assumed that they were about to be sent against the Indians.

South of the Ohio and between the Mississippi and the Appalachians—that is, what now comprises the states of Kentucky and Tennessee plus the northern two thirds of Alabama and Mississippi—was the area known as the Southwest Territory. Indians did not roam in those parts; they were settled, in a thousand tiny villages, and they were classed by the federal government as "civilized," which meant that some of them had gone in for farming, although hunting was still their principal occupation. Virtually all of them belonged to the Muskogean family and spoke more or less the same language. The white man called all of them Creeks—originally, it is supposed, because of the many small rivers in their territory.

The Creeks only gave the appearance of being closely knit, though. In fact, they were divided into northern and southern Creeks, and there were several offshoots or subsidiary tribes—the Chickasaws, the Cherokees, the Chickamaugas, and the Choctaws. Once, before they had been massacred almost to the last man by the French, the Natchez had been considered Muskogees, although certainly they came of different stock. Then too there was a spin-off tribe of the southern Creeks that had crossed the Spanish boundary into Florida and decided to remain there: these were Seminoles, the People Who Camped Far Away.

What has all this got to do with the outbreak of war in 1812? A great deal.

The Indians in the Southwest Territory numbered about 53,000, and they were strewn over more than 33,000,000 acres, much of it in the so-called Black Belt of Mississippi and Alabama, the richest soil in the world. Planters in the Carolinas, whose estates were worn out because of an unvarying growth of cotton, greedily eyed as potentially profitable these transmontane acres. So did many Georgians, who never had accepted the federal government's recognition of the Creek nation as a legitimate people, and who, additionally, never had given up their claims to land as far west as the Mississippi River. And so too, of course, did the speculators in Kentucky, Tennessee, and elsewhere, whose very mouths must have watered at the sight. Think of what could be done with 33,000,000 acres! Think of how it might be parceled and bought and sold and exchanged and mortgaged!

There was the immeasurably vast Louisiana territory on the other side of the Father of Waters, frontiersmen pointed out. Why not send the Creeks there, where they could not be forcibly moved? The government did indeed *urge* these Indians to make such a trek, offering them tracts of barren plains by the side of which their 33,000,000 acres would have looked like a woodlot.

The frontiersman, John Buckskin, did not think that urging was enough. Kick the bastards out, he said. Matters pertaining to treaties and to land titles could be settled afterward.

Were the Muskogees really "civilized"? Could they be considered an agricultural people? Their friends in Washington, those who sent missionaries among them, the Quakers, the Baptists, the Presbyterians, strove to convince the government that this great alteration was taking place. The Indians, these well-wishers said, needed to practice farming *and* hunting during the difficult time of the changeover, and that was why they needed all that land.

Tommyrot! cried the speculators. The land was simply going to waste, while men who might have made it into a valuable national property, the real farmers, were kept out because of a treaty they had not helped to frame, and in the execution of which they had no say.

"Look at the Iroquois," cried the Baptists, the Presbyterians, the Quakers. But this was an unfortunate suggestion and harmful to their own cause. The Iroquois, the once dreaded Six Nations—Mohawks, Senecas, Oneidas, Onondagas, Cayugas, Tuscaroras—had been the very epitome of the bestial savage, the bloodiest, cruelest, sneakiest redskins of them all, who only took to agriculture when they were forced to do so. They made poor farmers, and that had only caused them to be the more dependent upon the white men, who now enormously outnumbered them. When they had no wilderness to disappear into, when they were settled, the Iroquois could be threatened with extinction by starvation, as General Sullivan had proved in the last years of the Revolution, when he marched back and forth across western New York, burning their villages and their stores of grain. Was this civilization?

Now you take these Creeks. They were no farmers, the settlers avowed. They had learned to plant corn and cotton, but they were savages just the same. They still took scalps and hung them in their homes to dry. They still slow-burned prisoners in public places.

Not so, not so, protested the Presbyterians, the Baptists, the Quakers.

There was yet another voice in this long debate, although it was a muted one. At one time the French from Canada had controlled the fur trade in those parts. The French had moved easily among the Indians, dressed like them, learned their languages, helped them in their wars. Now the French were gone. Spain for a long time had claimed much of the Creek territory as a part of West Florida, but the Spaniards from New Orleans, though they tried, were not numerous enough or pliable enough to control the fur trade. Neither were the English, nor the Americans, who came in increasing numbers across the mountains from the Atlantic seaboard.

Those who took the place of the *coureurs de bois* were, unexpectedly, the Scots. Based in the Floridas or in the Bahama Islands, these canny traders mixed with the Indians in their own villages, and on a scale never reached by the French. They even intermarried with them, and their sons, half-breeds, became important Creek chiefs—Hoboi-Hili-Miko, or Alexander Mc-Gillivray, the "King of the Creeks," "the Alabama Talleyrand," was half Scottish, a quarter French, a quarter Indian—who saw to it that their relatives got all the business. Naturally these men, Scots fathers and half-breed sons alike, encouraged the Creeks to hold onto their lands at all costs. Naturally, too, they did it quietly and under cover. If war ever did come, they were prepared to keep their red friends supplied with guns and powder, as well as advice.

When the United States at last declared war on Great Britain, it announced that it did so in defense of "Free Trade and Sailors' Rights," even though New England, the trade leader of the nation and the section with the most sailors, was opposed to such a declaration and was to remain against the war.

Nobody was fooled. Land was the real reason. The two principal "war hawks," those who did most to force the conflict, were Henry Clay, a Westerner, and John C. Calhoun, a Southerner. The men of the Northwest Territory for many years had been eyeing with avarice the vast empty expanse of Canada, a land they believed the United States could easily take over—so long as Great Britain remained engaged in a death struggle with France on the continent of Europe. The Southerners, in their turn, fervently wished for an excuse to annex the Floridas, East and West. This was not because they looked forward to added material for land speculation, and certainly not because they sought another settlement site—who would want to settle in that flat, hot country?—but rather because they wished to close an escape hatch against their runaway slaves, whom the Spaniards were wont to befriend, and because they wished to forestall a British takeover. The Southwest Territory men also favored a war because they too were greedy for more land—in their case, the Creek lands, which could be confidently and legally stolen once the secret British influence was removed.

That is why when Andrew Jackson and all his men were called to arms early in the conflict, they assumed, at first, that they would be sent against the Creeks.

It came as a shock when their marching orders instructed them to go to New Orleans instead, to join the regular army forces under James Wilkinson.

Wilkinson was unspeakable. He was fat, a bigmouth, a blowhard, a crook. For years, when Spain still owned Louisiana, he had secretly accepted a Spanish pension, and in this capacity, as a spy, an informer, while acting as commander in chief of the U.S. Army in the West, he had tried again and again to goad the Creeks into revolt against their American masters. He wasn't even a good soldier. He had conspired at long distance with Aaron Burr to invade the Mexican state of Texas, perhaps even Mexico proper, where they planned to set up an independent military empire. But at the last minute, when Burr was drawing near with his ragamuffin array, Wilkinson had panicked and betrayed his partner to the authorities in Washington. Furthermore, Wilkinson had made the long trip by sea from New Orleans to Richmond, Virginia, where he testified against Burr, lying prodigiously, as the state's star witness. It was there that Jackson, who testified for Burr, met Wilkinson. Jackson detested him. But now Jackson was under orders to serve as Wilkinson's assistant. It must have been a bitter pill to swallow.

They started for New Orleans. In flatboats assembled by the commander in chief in a whirlwind campaign of acquisition, they were floated down the Tennessee, down the Ohio, down the Mississippi itself as far as Natchez, about halfway to New Orleans. There a dispatch carrier caught up with them.

The War Department had changed its mind. It had decided that neither New Orleans nor any part of the Gulf Coast was now threatened by the British. Wilkinson had been taken away from the Crescent City and was now being assigned to the command of a second invasion of Canada (the first had been an expensive failure). General Jackson was ordered to take his men home and there to disband them.

This was easier said than done. There were no steamboats on the Mississippi yet, and to pole those flatboats all the way back against the current was unthinkable. It would have taken many months, and supplies for such a trip were not available. They would have to go back overland, by way of the notoriously difficult Natchez Trace. But supplies for that trek were not available either. Andrew Jackson had to raise money on his own note, pledging the Hermitage and everything else he owned, a lifetime's savings, in order to buy sufficient food and medical supplies. (He was to get it back from the government eventually, years later, but at the time he made the deal, the way the war was going, it looked as thought there might not *be* any United States government in a little while.)

Anything but kindly, Jackson always was solicitous about his men. He saw to it that they were properly fed and that the sick were cared for, and that they all got their pay on time. The men appreciated that, but most of their admiration was for his tenacity, his durability. He could sure take it. It was known that he was painfully ill all this while and at times could hardly hold himself upright in the saddle; yet he seemed never to sleep. He led the men personally through the hardest places, and he listened to every complaint. It was at this time that they began to call him after the toughest wood that they knew. They called him Old Hickory.

Back in Nashville, and back in private life, he was once more involved in a duel. This one was to become a gold mine for the makers of bawdy ballads.

There was a young officer under his command, a man named Carroll, who had lately come from Virginia. Jackson liked him, but Carroll's messmates didn't—they thought him uppity—and one of them challenged. Carroll refused to accept the challenge on the ground that the man, though an officer, was no gentleman. Another man from the same company sent another challenge, and this too Carroll refused to accept, for the same reason. They were evidently out to get him, willy-nilly, into the field, because a third challenger promptly popped up.

This one was a youngster named Jesse Benton, a brother of General Jackson's good friend Colonel Thomas Hart Benton, and you didn't spurn a Benton with impunity. Carroll accepted. He asked Andrew Jackson to act for him.

Jackson at first refused. He was getting a bit old for such goings-on. Besides, both men were officers in his command, and it was not correct for him to represent one against the other. But Captain Carroll could not get anybody else to be his second, and Jackson at last agreed.

There had been much shaking of heads and clucking of tongues about the Jackson-Dickinson duel some years back, in part because Jackson had twisted his body around beneath that long cloak, in part because of the murderously short distance— eight paces. The terms of the Carroll-Benton duel, however, were really shocking. The men were to be placed back to back, their shoulder blades touching. At a signal they should step apart, turning to fire whenever they wished. Obviously neither would take a second step, lest he get a bullet in the back.

Young Benton sought to offset this closeness by squatting as he took his one stride. He turned only halfway toward his adversary, and he was very low, almost pressing the ground, when he fired. From that cramped position he missed. Carroll, disconcerted to find his foe seemingly crouched at his feet, was wild. His ball did hit Jesse Benton, but not in a vital spot. Benton's behind was outthrust—in profile, as it were, to the man with the pistol. It was a natural target. Carroll's bullet ripped open the seat of a good pair of trousers and tore a nasty gash out of each of the protruding buttocks.

Benton couldn't sit down for weeks. He was, of course, the laughingstock of Tennessee.

If either Andrew Jackson or Thomas Hart Benton had had a sense of humor, the business might have ended right there, but neither did. Colonel Benton got the idea that Jackson was somehow the cause of it all. He wrote sharply to Jackson, who wrote sharply back. Soon, egged on by friends, the two were calling each other all sorts of names. General Jackson swore that if and when Colonel Benton came back to Nashville (he was in Washington on army business) he would seek him out and horsewhip him.

Colonel Benton did come back, and he and his kid brother took a room in a Nashville inn not ordinarily patronized by Andrew Jackson. Jackson, a walking stick in one hand, a loaded pistol under his coat, went looking for them. He was accompanied by another friend, who was similarly equipped, Colonel John Coffee. Coffee, like Jackson himself, was a Donelson by marriage; he was the husband of one of Rachel's nieces.

Thomas Hart Benton was alone, lounging in the open doorway of his hotel, when Andrew Jackson returned from the post office. Jackson flew at him, cane raised, pistol out. Benton stepped back into a hallway, Jackson after him. Then Benton stopped in another open doorway, from which steps led down to the cellar.

It happened very fast. A hall door to Jackson's right was thrown open, and Jesse Benton emerged from a bedroom, pistol in hand. Seeing his brother about to be shot, Jesse shot the general, who fell to the floor, a ball in his left shoulder.

At this moment Colonel Coffee came charging in from the street, a pistol in *his* hand. He fired at Colonel Benton, who, startled, stepped backward—and fell down the cellar steps. A Jacksonite whose name has not survived came in from the street right behind Coffee, and he saw Jesse Benton with a smoking pistol, so he knocked him down and started to stamp on his face with hobnailed boots, a common practice in those parts.

This unlovely performance caused the patched-up Bentons to decide that Tennessee was no longer a good place for them, and they moved to Missouri. Andrew Jackson was still alive, though barely. He had lost a lot of blood, and was laid up for several weeks. When he did rise, swaying, it was again at the call of his country. The Creeks were on the warpath at last.

He staggered into action.

4
IN TIME FOR TEA

"Why does Jackson kill so many Indians?" somebody asked Governor Blount.

"Because he knows how," the Governor replied.

Here was no flapping-banners war, no clash of masses featured by jingling sabretaches, the boom of brass cannons, high-flourished swords. Here was a contest marked by sneakiness and attack from the back, a dark, dirty affair conducted in the semisecrecy of shadows.

The American Indian north of the Rio Grande never had learned to look upon war as a formal exercise, a move this way to counteract a move that way, a shuttling, a connection immediately followed by a disconnection. The ambush he knew well, the siege not at all. He might flee, and often did, but he had no talent for retreat. All, to him, was blood and ferocity, shrieks and scalps; all was hit and run. He knew nothing of parades, drills, mock war exercises. Neither was defense fighting for him. Whenever the resistance got rough he disappeared.

This suited Andrew Jackson. He too liked violence. He had never been one to pull punches.

It would be, both sides understood, a no-prisoner war.

The Creek territory was vast and full of many swamps in which Indians could hide, but Jackson had Creeks of his own to act as scouts who could find them out and trap them. The whole campaign was a seek-and-destroy operation. Jackson's young militiamen were well armed, while the Indians were short of muskets and powder. The Scottish traders had kept them supplied with enough arms to make the hunting worthwhile, to keep the pelts coming in, but this war had caught them by surprise and once Jackson had taken the field they were unable to contact their dusky friends.

Three times Jackson's troops cornered the enemy, and three times there was a massacre. The Creek women and children, if they kept quiet, ordinarily were spared; the men never. It was bloody, nasty work, but it didn't last long. After the third major slaughter, at Horseshoe Bend, the Creeks sued.

Andrew Jackson made the peace terms as harsh as he dared. He did not seize *all* of the Creek territory, for such a dictate Washington would have reversed, but out there in the field, in the wilderness, he reduced this nation to extreme poverty, leaving it no hope that it might ever get back its old-time glory. Then Jackson inquired, circuitously, about the possibility of a commission in the regular army. He had been thinking about it for some time, for he had learned that he liked the military life; he enjoyed being a general.

Washington responded with unaccustomed promptitude. He could be appointed a brigadier general in the U.S. Army. There was no major generalship vacant.

The Hammer of the Creeks pondered this as he was making preparations to return to the Hermitage. He would have *preferred* a major general's stars, of course, but still, at the same time . . .

In a fit of pique, something to do with precedence, Major General William Henry Harrison threw up his commission, and the War Department hastily sent an offer of it to Andrew Jackson, who hastily accepted.

Thus, a man who had never served a day in the army became one of its highest-ranking officers. He was put in charge of the

Seventh Military District, roughly the same as the Southwest Territory.

The war was going badly for the United States. The Canadian militia had cracked all expectations by electing to fight, and it fought well. The first invasion had been hurled back, and the second, under the malodorous Wilkinson, had been even more emphatically trounced. The Royal Navy, though all the while blockading France and the French holdings in the Low Countries, nevertheless had enough seaworthy ships left over to seal off the entire Atlantic coast of the United States. Now and then a frigate slipped out to fight spectacularly with its British counterpart off the coast, and individual privateers were making themselves a nuisance to the British West Indian trade, but most American war vessels, shorn of their guns, had been towed as far up sundry rivers as they would go—to places where the British warships, with their heavy hardware, could not follow them—and there been abandoned or burned.

A British amphibian force had struck at will in the Chesapeake region. The capital itself had been taken, and the White House burned. Bonaparte, his Grande Armée bled white by the Russian adventure, had capitulated, and was presently a pampered prisoner on the island of Elba; and that meant the release for action in farther fields of the cream of the British army, the crack regiments, which were now being rested and re-equipped. A huge British fleet was assembling off Negril Point, the western tip of Jamaica, and there seemed little doubt that these regiments would be sent there for use against some strategic place in the United States, probably New Orleans.

The War Department in Washington became alarmed. After all, control of the Crescent City meant control of the mouths of the Mississippi, of the whole river. So Washington was delighted to learn that Andrew Jackson would consent to accept a command in the regular army. He was promptly assigned to defend New Orleans.

Jackson went to Mobile. The alacrity with which he made this leap suggests that he had already decided that Mobile would be the British target. Mobile (now in Alabama) was in West Florida, which of course was Spanish, but the Spaniards and the British were allies for the moment, and anyway the British had been using Florida pretty much as they pleased for many years, knowing that the weak dons could do nothing about it.

Mobile could be made to serve as the base for a full-fledged attack upon New Orleans. It was much nearer to the mouths of the Mississippi than was Negril Point, though it was vulnerable to attack by land. Or Mobile could become the place for unloading the whole army, which thereafter would march overland to New Orleans.

Jackson favored the second possibility. He did not seem aware of the difficulties of marching a modern army—the soldiers and marines, the collapsible bridges, the gunsmiths, the blacksmiths, the fieldpieces, the horses, the fodder, the rations, and the mountainous supplies of shot and powder—over almost two hundred miles of sand and watery wilderness. It would be Mobile, he was sure, so he went there, and he stayed a long time, examining the defenses of the place and ignoring the letters from New Orleaneans, who were hopping with anxiety.

Even when he heard that British war vessels had been sighted off the mouths of the Mississippi, and that British naval officers had approached the smuggler-pirates of Barataria Bay in search of river pilots—even then he did not believe it. That, he wrote to his friend John Coffee (himself a general now, and busy raising troops back in Tennessee), was just a "faint." When he got to New Orleans at last and it was reported to him that a Lieutenant Colonel Edward Nicholls of the British army, who was ashore at Pensacola trying to enlist Indian scouts, had publicly predicted that his nation's military forces would be in the Crescent City within two months, Andrew Jackson only snorted. "There will be bloody noses before that happens," he said.

New Orleans would be a great prize. It was crammed to

the last inch of warehouse space with cotton, millions of dollars worth, that the planters in those parts could not ship away because of the blockade. The residents were afraid that General Jackson would order the whole city burned to the ground rather than allow this immense fortune to fall into the hands of the enemy. It was just the sort of thing that he might do, from what they had heard about him.

The city was more than a hundred miles from the open Gulf of Mexico, and the intervening country on both sides of the river was treacherous, shifting, squashy—a maze of quaking prairies, bayous, dead-end waterways, and cypress swamp. With its pelicans and herons, cranes, flamingos, and kingfishers, with its mallards and pintails and teal, its 'possum and 'gator and otter and bear, its gar and bream, and black bass, perch, sunnies, mudfish, it could have been huzzahed as a sportsman's paradise. But it was no place for an army with a siege train.

The Mississippi had five main mouths, and the deepest of these granted only twelve feet at the bar. It was protected by an old fort at Belize, but that could be knocked out, if indeed it was still standing. Even so, the large vessels, the ones heavily laden with guns, and the transports, could not get in.

About fifty miles upstream, at an angle, Fort St. Philip and Fort Bourbon faced each other across the river. Neither amounted to much, according to British intelligence, and Fort Bourbon when last reported on was no more than a ruin. Still, they might have been rebuilt and rearmed, regarrisoned too, if this man Jackson knew his business.

Even farther up, barely sixteen miles below the city itself, was the worst place of all, English Turn. Here the twist in the stream was such that for about three and a half miles it actually flowed north and sailing craft—the British had no galleys—even with luck would be held up for at least a few hours under the guns of a fort that surely would be in good condition, Jackson or no Jackson.

But there were other ways of getting there.

Close to the Mississippi's mouths, on the west side, was a route made up of Bayou Pointe au Chien and the Bayou aux Boeufs, which would float a man clear up to English Turn, but he would have to be a man in a very small boat and he couldn't hope to carry any cannon.

West of the mouths there were two principal routes. Bayou La Fourche started at the Gulf about eight miles from the westernmost mouth. It was navigable but narrow, and could easily be defended. Barataria Bay, between Bayou La Fourche and the river, had a channel ten feet deep, which extended for seventy miles directly north, and after that was broken into a series of bayous, small streams, and swamps, by means of which, if you had the right guide, you could reach a point on the west bank of the Mississippi right opposite New Orleans. But guides were not available in those parts just then.

Barataria for years had been controlled by smugglers, whose headquarters at Grande Terre recently had been raided by federal forces who had arrested one of their two brother-leaders, Pierre Lafitte, a fat, slow, cross-eyed blacksmith. The other brother, Jean, was even then in the city, a fugitive, seeking an audience with General Jackson, with whom he hoped to make a deal: Pierre's freedom and pardon, in return for which the smuggler chiefs would lend Jackson a couple of fieldpieces together with the gunners to handle them.

So the western routes could be crossed out.

East of Au Chien a series of small islands hugged the Gulf Coast, forming a sound that stretched all the way to Mobile. This in fact was an avenue of coasting trade between the two cities. The western tip of this sound was formed by Lake Borgne, which really is a very shallow lagoon, opening into a labyrinth of bayous and eventually into Lake Pontchartrain, the back door of New Orleans. This seemed the most likely approach. There were various watery passages between Lake Borgne and Lake Pontchartrain, but all were narrow and shallow, and while not fortified could easily be blocked. Jackson had ordered that trees be chopped down across all of them.

He did not believe that the British would come by way of Lake Pontchartrain. He believed that they would take a longer but less aqueous route, the Chef Menteur road, and it was there that he massed most of the forces at his command.

These forces were motley. The commander of the Seventh Military District had only sixty marines and two regiments of regulars, the 44th and the 7th, armed with muskets, not rifles, besides a heterogeneous collection of militiamen and dashing if inexperienced guards volunteers, few of them well armed. He had perhaps two thousand men in all, but he was increasing his force all the time.

Jackson declared martial law in New Orleans, suspending the habeas corpus. He accepted the services of a regiment of "free men of color," and armed them, to the consternation of the Creoles, who believed that nobody with a drop of Negro blood in his veins should be permitted even to touch a firearm. He made a deal with the younger Lafitte, whereby the commander in chief issued pardons for both brothers in return for the services of two artillery teams complete with fieldpieces, powder, and even some ball. He examined the city's defenses everywhere, and greatly strengthened them along the Chef Menteur road.

At about noon of December 23, a hot muggy day, the advance guard of what was known for the occasion as the 22nd Light Brigade, an elite British outfit consisting of 1,688 rank and file, stepped out of the swamp at the edge of the Villeré plantation on the east bank of the river.

These men had just spent the past four days and nights in the swamp. It had rained most of the time, and it had been cold. At the western tip of Lake Borgne they had come upon a village of fishermen, Spaniards, who could speak no English.

But there were officers among the British, veterans of the Peninsular War, who were fluent in Spanish, and the fishermen had no feeling of loyalty for the Yanquis who had recently taken over this part of the world. For a trifle of money they had gladly informed the visitors that this particular bayou, a remote one named Bienvenu, unaccountably had not been blocked by trees like the others, and was unguarded.

The fishermen had then gone fishing, and the officers who had elicited this interesting information from them had returned to the Isle aux Pois to fetch the rest of the advance forces. While they were gone a picket of one sergeant and eight privates of the U.S. Army had taken over the deserted village. These men, tired after a long pole through Bayou Bienvenu, promptly stretched out for a sleep, having posted no sentries. The British had come back from Isle aux Pois in overwhelming force and without the firing of a shot or even the raising of a voice, had taken them prisoner. Then the British had proceeded along Bayou Bienvenu in their tiny shallow-draft boats until they came out upon the Villeré plantation.

Not one American soldier was in sight. There were no entrenchments, there was no fortification.

New Orleans was only nine miles—*dry* miles—to the north. The British could be there in time for tea.

This was the hour of the siesta, and nothing moved, not even a butterfly, on the plantation, which was owned by General Villeré, the commanding officer of the Louisiana militia. Yes; there was one movement! On the veranda of the plantation house, in a chair, his feet on the railing, a handkerchief over his face, sat a lithe young man. It was the handkerchief that stirred. It went up and down . . . up and down . . . rhythmically . . . .

The sleeper was Gabriel Villeré, the son of the owner. Gabriel was a major in the militia, but he was not wearing his uniform. The British thought it might be well to question him. Politely, quietly, they awakened the lad.

Gabriel sat up, gawping, and the handkerchief slithered from his face. He saw all the strangers who had overrun the plantation, and he thought fast. As somnolence flopped from him, he sprang to his feet, wrenched himself loose from the intruders, vaulted the veranda rail, and got out of there.

He sped north, but when he heard them following him he veered to the right, plunging into the swamp.

The soldiers did not pursue. They knew better than to venture back in without a guide.

Their well-founded fear of the swamp was not the only reason these intruders did not keep after young Villeré. The 22nd Light Brigade was in the charge of Lieutenant Colonel William Thornton. Thornton was an energetic soldier, but it would hardly do for a mere colonel to capture an enemy capital when the main force contained no fewer than four generals. The chief of these, Sir Edward Pakenham, delayed by the bad weather that had plagued the expedition from the start, was expected any day. Pakenham was a brother-in-law of the Duke of Wellington, no less, and it was common knowledge that he had in his wallet a proclamation creating him Earl of Louisiana and military governor-general thereof, to be issued when New Orleans was taken.

Thornton was anything but a cautious man, but the situation smelled strange to him. It could be a trap. The approach had been too easy, the way too smooth. The prisoners in the fishing village had averred that Jackson commanded at least twenty thousand men, and while undoubtedly they had lied, twenty thousand was a figure to ponder and to respect. The plantation hands and the house servants now being questioned were saying the same thing. Also, the weather had worsened. The plantation had been drenched with sunshine when the brigade first burst upon it, but now the sky was overcast, the air was chill, and streamers of fog were drifting in from the river.

So it was that the British allowed young Villeré to go—and lost the war.

They badly needed a rest. They dug in, though only after taking the usual precautions, posting the usual pickets. The heroes of Vittoria, Badajoz, Salamanca, were not men to be caught off guard. They were not surprised, then, in the military sense, though they certainly were startled, when at about sundown—if there had been any sun—Andrew Jackson smashingly paid them a visit.

5
SLAUGHTER
IN THE DELTA

Gabriel Villeré had run the whole distance, pausing only for an instant to pick up a friend, Dussau de la Croix, who could speak some English, a language of which Villeré had not a word, and who would know how to find the headquarters of General Jackson.

Jackson had been in the city for three weeks, but the residents had seen little of him because he was furiously busy. Their first shock, when they beheld him at a formal reception, had been one of delight, because they had expected just another Kaintuck. To Creoles a Kaintuck, or Kentuckian, was anybody who came down the river—that is, a vulgar, vociferous flatboatman—but instead they saw an immaculate soldier who was courtly of manner, and the Creoles admired courtliness. Jackson, however, showed himself very little after that first night. He was no balcony ranter, no bower to applause. When he wasn't on a whirlwind inspection of the outlying defenses he was at his headquarters, 135 Royal Street, a place hard to get into.

Villeré and De la Croix were admitted, though, and one gasped out his amazing tale while the other, also panting heavily, tried to interpret. But De la Croix was so excited that he forgot most of the English he knew, which was broken at best, and since nobody on the premises knew a word of French it looked

49

for a little while as though the British would be given all the time they needed to take the city. Then a bilingual person, a passerby, was called in from the street.

Andrew Jackson summoned no council. He examined no notes. He rose, strapping on his sword.

"My God, gentlemen," he cried, "we'll fight them right now!"

They slambanged down the east bank to the Plain of Chalmette, and as soon as they saw the gleam of campfires through the fog and heard the blurred popping of muskets that sentries fired, they charged.

"We'll give them a little Christmas fandango," said Andrew Jackson, though it was only the twenty-third, Christmas Eve eve.

It was a curious sort of battle, eerie. The redcoats, though their limbs ached and their backs were sore, sprang from their blankets and reached for their guns. But just at first they did not take this attack seriously. Who in his right mind would hurl raw levies across an open plain against an entrenched force of veterans as night was falling? The redcoats assumed that this was a scouting party of Jackson's Dirty Shirts that in the fog had stumbled into the British camp and was raising a hullaballoo only in order to bat their way out.

The Americans, fiercely, like men afire, opposed the British bayonets with their own long rifles. The confusion was terrible. Since there was no breeze to blow it away the gun smoke hung in the air, mixing with the mist, which had thickened and was writhing low in languid, baffled coils. The flashes of musket fire lit a fantastic scene. Men kept getting lost—alone, in pairs, in groups.

Still, the British did not break, and indeed they began to press forward.

Jackson then did something he must have hated to do. He ordered a retreat.

The British did not pursue. They'd had enough for one night, and after posting fresh pickets they went back to their blankets. It was the common belief among the officers, from Thornton down, that those Yankee regulars back in the fishing village had told the truth after all, for Jackson, they reasoned, must have had at least twenty thousand troops to launch an attack like that. It would be better to wait until General Keane came up with the main body of the expedition.

The official figures—dead, wounded, missing—were: British 46, 167, 64; American 24, 115, 74.

It had been *magnifique* all right, even if it had not been *la guerre*.

Jackson fell back as far as the Rodriguez Canal, an irrigation ditch about ten feet wide and three quarters of a mile long, extending from the river to the swamp, into which it emptied. Because of the lowness of the Mississippi there was no water in the Rodriguez Canal that night, though the bottom was goo.

Jackson's plan was to attack again at dawn, and only with difficulty did his aides talk him out of it. Instead, he ordered up reinforcements and set all his men to work building a breast-work on the northern lip of the canal, the side toward the city. This breastwork, which was to become famous, was made chiefly of earth. There were no rocks in that part of the world. Some wood was cut in the swamp and some lumber was brought down from New Orleans, but it was buried deep in the wall for fear of flying splinters.

The freighter *Pallas*, destined for Havana but anchored in the Mississippi because of the blockade, contributed 277 bales of cotton. A few of these bales were embedded into the breast-work at one point, but it was soon learned that they caught fire easily from the flintlocks, musket, and rifle alike, that the defenders used. A smoldering bale of cotton was extremely hard to put out, and customarily, when that happened, the men dumped the whole thing down into the ditch, where it continued to smolder, throwing smoke up into their eyes, while the bale itself covered and neutralized the caltrops.

Caltrops—sometimes called crows' feet—were iron balls to each of which four spikes were fastened in such a way that when the thing was thrown to the ground one spike remained upright. Their only function was to discourage cavalry. Why any had been issued to the U.S. Army in the Delta is a mystery, but as long as they were there—there weren't many of them anyway—it was decided to strew them along the bottom of the Rodriguez Canal.

The remaining bales of cotton, the great majority, were used in emergency lines of defense, of which there were three, and in the construction of gun emplacements.

Thornton, Jackson's Choctaw scouts told him, was making preparations to receive reinforcements, and he already had, in a well-laid-out and fortified camp, the 85th, the 95th, a company of one hundred sappers, a company of rocketeers, and the 4th Foot.

The Congreve rocket was the "secret weapon" of the War of 1812. A failure at first, it had seemed to prove its efficacy in several naval engagements, though not in the attack on Fort McHenry, where it made a lot of noise and inspired Francis Scott Key, an onlooker, to write the line "The rockets' red glare, the bombs bursting in air," but did little else. Now it was to be tried for the first time in battle, because this weapon and the men specially trained to handle it were a part of the Royal Artillery, and were supposed to operate on land. It was purely a fright machine, to be used *in terrorem,* and this should be a good place for it, the invaders believed, since it was well known that the Americans scared easily.

The rocket tubes, or troughs, before the Rodriguez line were sited some distance back, behind the siege guns. There were six of them, and they were built to fire 32-pound rockets, the biggest. They were placed far back so that their flights would describe a bigger arc and spew more dreadful black smoke, but also because the regular artillerists, the conventional ones, were afraid of the damned things.

A Congreve rocket consisted of a 3½-foot metal head fastened to a 15-foot wooden guiding stick—a huge skyrocket, in fact. It was filled with black powder and fitted with a long fuse. It carried the stick with it when it was fired.

In addition, the British had four 24-pound howitzers, two field batteries of four 9-pounders each, and a siege train made up of ten long 12-pounders.

Opposing this armament the Americans had a heterogeneous collection of cannon that was technically superior to the British, at least in the amount of metal it could throw, but actually weaker, because it consisted of six different types of guns with five different calibers. There were an iron 32-pound carronade, which had a terrific recoil but wouldn't carry far; three long iron 24-pounders; one Spanish long brass 18-pounder; one U.S. Navy long iron 18-pounder; three French brass 12-pounders; six American brass 6-pounders, which were of no use at all at that distance; and one 10-inch mortar, which could not be fired because the Americans had no time fuses for its shells. Besides, there were the guns of the U.S.S. *Caroline* and the U.S.S. *Louisiana*, in the river near the west bank, and a battery of 18-pounders on the opposite shore. These guns, obliged to fire clear across the Mississippi, could, in the beginning of the campaign, cause the British left wing to cling flat against the levee but could not threaten the main body of the invaders.

Sir Edward Pakenham, a major general, arrived on the scene on Christmas Day. He was thirty-eight and in perfect health (Jackson was forty-eight and suffering horribly from dysentery), and he did not like what he saw. Granted, the advance guard had done a brilliant job in reaching this spot all undetected and unharmed, but once the American general had plugged the hole, what else was there to do? The Americans had only five miles of road—and it *was* road, hard-packed—to their base. The British were eighty-odd miles, all water, from *their* base, the fleet.

The two sides were about equal in the number of fighting men, but the Americans could still be reinforced, whereas the British had brought up all of their available troops. The British staff officers had mounts, of course, but there were no pack animals. They had expected to pick these up on the scene, but they were disappointed. The Americans had plenty of horses and some mules as well.

Part of the British plan had been to enlist large numbers of Creek Indians as scouts, as flank coverers, but the Creeks had been thoroughly cowed in the recent war in the wilderness and were not available. The Americans had Choctaws, who haunted the swamp, shadows that carried long knives. The Americans penetrated the swamp at will to cut cypress branches, which they wove into gabions, wickerwork baskets open at both ends and stuffed with mud, of which there was always plenty; they used these "cribs" in their temporary fortifications. The British could not do this.

The British soldiers had to do all their own digging, a tremendous job in that mushy, wobbly land. The Americans had a seemingly unlimited supply of slave labor, Negroes lent by planters and by the residents of New Orleans. At one time it was estimated that there two thousand slaves in the American camp, almost as many men as lined the canal.

In other words, time was on the side of the Americans. All they had to do was stand pat. It was up to the Britishers to do something, and the longer they waited, the harder that something would be.

General Pakenham did not at first even consider a frontal attack. His right wing was blocked by that terrible swamp, into which his men could not be driven. The American left wing, as a matter of fact, extended deep into the swamp, though it is not likely that Pakenham knew it. His left wing was being peppered from the gunboats and the long toms on the opposite bank.

Pakenham ordered the four howitzers emplaced on the levee and he set up the two huge furnaces he had brought with him to heat the balls. Cold balls could do little harm at that distance, but a well-placed hot shot might. He was lucky. After only a few minutes of firing, men were seen to be jumping off the *Carolina* and desperately swimming to shore. Then the boat blew up, a total loss. A heated cannonball had torn right into her magazine. The *Louisiana* was towed to safety—there wasn't a breath of wind—by smallboatmen who rowed through a rain of balls that hissed when they hit the water. She was anchored at last under the guns of the makeshift fort, whose guns at about that same time knocked out two of Pakenham's howitzers. From there the *Louisiana* could no longer reach the British left wing, though she could still make an advance upon the canal a perilous move.

Pakenham ordered Colonel Thornton to knock out the battery on the other side of the river.

The Earl-elect of Louisiana next tried a reconnaissance in force. At least that's what he called it in his report. Andrew Jackson called it a battle.

The morning of the twenty-eighth was a clear day for a change. The British, formed into two beautiful brigades, marched toward the American line. They halted at last, well out of the range of the American rifles, but within the range of the field guns, which immediately opened fire. The redcoats did not shoot but simply stood there. Now and then one would crumple to the ground, but his companions never even glanced at him. The officers conferred. Then suddenly the soldiers turned, no doubt on command, and, in flawless order, picked up their wounded and dead—about forty in number—and marched away.

It was a superb demonstration of cold courage, of iron

discipline, though what it had proved would be hard to say.

Next, General Pakenham decreed that there should be an artillery duel. The British gunners were the best in the world, and they should have no trouble knocking out their opposite numbers on the other side of the Rodriguez Canal. Besides, this would be the *correct* way to proceed with the campaign. Everybody knew that each arm of the military service should engage and defeat its corresponding arm on the enemy side before a full-scale engagement was joined.

Neither side had cavalry. A clash of infantry would call for a frontal attack on the part of the British. And the Americans, most of them anyway, had rifles.

The rifle had been a German invention. When Germans—the mercenaries from Hesse-Cassel, Hesse-Hanau, Brunswick, Anspach-Bayreuth, Waldeck, and Anhalt-Zerbst—had been brought over as "auxiliaries" in the American Revolution, they had their jaegers, most of them former gamekeepers or woodsmen (the name means "huntsmen"), who wore green coats, carried rifles, and were used as snipers. These men learned that the rifle was already established in the emergent nation, having been constructed—or reconstructed?—by German gunsmiths who had settled in western Pennsylvania. It was what became the Kentucky rifle, though it should have been called the Pennsylvania rifle. The rifle was longer than the weapon the jaeger carried, though not as heavy, and was confined, in America, to the frontiersmen. Very few of these men got into Washington's Continental army. Those that did were used, as were the jaegers, largely as snipers. There were never many of them, because sniping, in those pre-smokeless-powder days, when shooting distances were so short, was an extremely perilous business. The rank-and-file infantryman carried a musket, which was the weapon for battles, for formal as distinguished from guerilla warfare.

Military men were reluctant to adopt the rifle. The musket

was a more reliable weapon, easier to reload, easier to keep clean. Even in the War of 1812 the American infantryman, like his British counterpart, carried a musket.

The rifle had a very long barrel, which was needed to give the ball the right spin. That meant it could not be reloaded from a kneeling position, an important consideration in open fighting. It meant also that, *being* rifled, it took much longer to reload, to tamp down the powder, the ball, the wadding, with a long ramrod. All infantry tactics were still based on controlled firepower; all shooting was done by volley, on command; and here the musket was superior. The rifle, granted, could shoot much more accurately, and it could shoot twice as far—roughly, it could kill at two hundred yards—but it would not shoot as fast. Defenders with muskets could get in a second volley before their assailants could close with them. Riflemen could not do that. Also, you couldn't fasten a bayonet on a rifle; it made the thing too long.

What regular army troops Jackson had were equipped with muskets, but most of his troops were militiamen from Tennessee, Kentucky, and Louisiana, and they carried rifles. General Pakenham knew this, and he knew that in a frontal assault the redcoats would be met by bullets long before they could get off a volley of their own, if they ever did. This was a contingency for which these robots had not been trained.

What Pakenham did not know was that the governors of Kentucky and Tennessee both had been sending south many troops who were unequipped with either muskets or rifles, for they were under the impression that the army had a surplus of firearms in storage in New Orleans. Even while Sir Edward was laying his plans, great numbers of Kaintuck reinforcements were tumbling out of their keelboats with nothing more to fight with than their hunting knives. "I don't believe it," Andrew Jackson cried when he heard. "I never met a man from Kentucky yet but he had a bottle of whiskey, a pack of cards, and a gun!"

At a quarter to eleven on the morning of New Year's Day, 1815, the fog lifted suddenly, dramatically, like the raising of a great curtain. The British were discovered in serried rows, their bayonets gleaming, just out of range of the Dirty Shirts' rifles, and back of them the gun crews stood by their well-stocked cannon.

The British opened up immediately, though their shots, from big guns, little guns, and rockets alike, were too high. They saw this, but could not seem to correct it.

The Americans, like a cool duelist, waited to take aim. They waited a good fifteen minutes. Then they opened up with everything they had. They were a great deal more accurate than their opponents. They concentrated on the siege guns, the 12-pounders, and soon they had knocked five of them out of action.

The Congreve rockets were an unmitigated flop. Like the cannon, and perhaps for the same reason—had somebody put a decimal point in the wrong place?—they persistently fired too high. They made a frightful noise and emitted clouds of black, stinking smoke, but they went well over the heads of the men they were supposed to intimidate, the men lining the north bank of the Rodriguez Canal. In fact, many of those men watched the flights while they laid bets as to where the silly thing would land, when they should have been keeping their eyes on the plain. However, the four thousand musketeers never did charge, and the rockets poofed out.

Days in advance the conventional artillerists had marked the Macarté house, a large, white, two-story wooden structure a few hundred feet north of the canal on a slight rise of ground. They had supposed, correctly, that this was the American general's field headquarters, and they hit it at least seventy times. But the General wasn't there. He was in the front line, examining the defenses, encouraging the men. So severe was his diarrhea that he couldn't sit a horse, and he hobbled from place to place, wincing in pain from time to time but never releasing a groan.

One of his aides carried a spade. Latrines were few and far between in that part of the field, and the General had to stop often to decorate the Louisiana mud. Many jokes were made about this defecation-and-inspection trip, which entered the folklore of those parts.

Others too were sick that day, but they were south of the canal.

The British needed material with which to build empaulments—the technical name for the breastworks built to protect gun crews—for they did not have bales of cotton, as did their American cousins. They did, however, have several hundred hogsheads of unrefined sugar they had found stored in the Villeré and Lacoste plantations, and they used them. The American cannonballs, so much more accurately fired than the British, soon battered the makeshift walls to shreds, and the rain got at their exposed contents, which became a thick, sticky, black stuff, full of grit and little splinters of cane. The cannoneers, half crazed with cold and hunger—they had been fed only ship's biscuit and a tot of rum since the previous day at sunset—gulped this viscous substance, and it made them sick. Every cot in the large field hospital was already filled, and these poor fellows had to lie out in the open, in the rain, vomiting violently.

Pakenham and his generals conferred, and they agreed that the royal forces had been decisively outgunned and that the only course left was a frontal attack.

This was made on January 8.

At ten minutes after five o'clock that misty morning—ten minutes late—General Pakenham gave the signal for the firing of a rocket that should tell Colonel Thornton on the other side of the river to start shooting.

It didn't, because Thornton was not there. He had been assigned the 5th West Indian, the 85th Regulars, two hundred seamen, and two hundred marines, and with these he was to cross the river under cover of night and assault the "fort" the

Americans under Master-Commander D. T. Patterson, U.S.N., had built around an old lime kiln, where a long tom battery threatened the British left. Besides his gunners, Patterson had a couple of hundred slaves, four hundred fifty Louisiana militiamen, and about two hundred unarmed Kaintucks.

The British, over on the east bank, had performed engineering wonders in an attempt to pierce the levee and float in from the Villeré Canal a fleet of small boats sufficient to carry Thornton's men to Patterson's position. The British engineers, naval men most of them, had never before encountered anything like the mud of the Delta country. The walls of the levee breech caved in again and again. The canal refused to fill. Rollers were brought up to try to work the boats toward the river, but the rollers sank out of sight. All of this had to be done in the dead of night, usually in a cold rain, for if Thornton's boats were spotted on the big stream they could be sunk by Patterson's guns or by the guns of the *Louisiana*, anchored just a little way upstream from the "fort." In fact, all guns and gunners had been stripped from the *Louisiana* for use elsewhere, but the British did not know that.

Four hours late, through no fault of his own, Thornton had got only a few boats, and he had taken off with only four hundred picked men. The current, which apparently he had not counted upon, kept him from reaching the "fort" in time, and he was still afloat, a few miles away, when the rocket signal was set off.

At just about that same time the mist lifted, and the Americans saw the plain before them fairly swarming with soldiers of the king. This did not startle them. They had expected it.

There were about 3,200 men in the canal line, as many as could be crowded in. Just behind them was an amateur band from New Orleans, which had been brought out for a New Year's celebration that never was held because of the artillery duel. The band promptly struck up "Yankee Doodle," one of the two numbers for which they had brought the music.

The Americans had built a *flèche,* an arrowhead-shaped breastwork, on the inner levee a little in advance of the Rodriguez Canal, the tip of their right wing. It was this that Thornton, using Patterson's guns, was supposed to knock out. Next to this *flèche* were stationed: the 7th, raw troops who had never before been under fire, and who carried muskets; then Plauche's battalion, gentlemen volunteers, the pride of New Orleans; then LaCosta's Santo Domingans and Daquin's free men of color, who made up the center; after that the Tennesseans, Jackson's own and Coffee's, who extended into the swamp, making up the American left wing. Between the two Tennessee outfits were a couple of hundred Kentuckians, who had rifles.

The British guns opened up; the American guns answered.

General Gibbs commanded the British right; General Keane, the left; General Lambert, who had close to 2,000 men, the rear. Gibbs had about 2,200 men in all, the 4th, 21st, 44th, and three companies of the 45th.

Keane, as ordered, struck at the *flèche.* His men took the place, but Beale's Rifles, blue-shirted volunteers, took it back, with some help from the neighboring 7th regiment.

Keane had the 93rd, two companies of the 95th, two companies of fusileers, and the 43rd, some 1,200 men in all.

About a quarter of the men in these forward units carried either scaling ladders or fascines. The fascines were heavy, bulky bundles of green sugarcane tied together with twine. They were to be dumped into the Rodriguez Canal. They never got there.

As soon as the American fieldpieces opened fire, Britiishers began falling, but only one or two at a time, here and there. The American gunners were using grape, scatter stuff. It was when Gibbs obliqued against the Kentuckians that the real slaughter started.

This movement brought the redcoats into the range of the rifles. It was like a continuous sheet of flame. Men fell in swathes, as though mowed down by some giant scythe. They broke, making for the swamp.

61

Keane, seeing that Gibbs was in trouble over there, dispatched the 93rd to his assistance. These were the Sutherlands, "the most Highland of the Highland regiments," in their brave green kilts, nine hundred rank and file. Something happened to them on the way to the right wing. Something terrible. They halted, no doubt on command. For a full five minutes they simply stood there, within easy reach of Kentuckians and Tennesseans alike, and the world learned how well Americans could shoot. The killing was terrible. Man after man crumpled like an empty potato sack, but the rest, stony-faced, did not stir. At last the difficulty, whatever it was, was straightened out, and an order was given for them to proceed toward the swamp. Only *a hundred and sixty* were able to do so.

Meanwhile, General Keane had been shot and killed. General Gibbs was hit four times, and he died, swearing furiously. General Pakenham spurred his horse forward to see if he could help. A ball caught him in the left forearm. His horse was downed, but he mounted another. A ball got him in the neck, knocking him out of the saddle, and before his aides could reach him, a chunk of grape tore open his right thigh, smashing a blood vessel, so that he died very quickly, bleeding to death there on the ground.

The American bandsmen struck up the other number they had brought, "Hail Columbia."

Pakenham's last words were an order to Lambert to bring up the reserves. Lambert, the only general left, looked around— and called for a retreat.

The whole business had taken about half an hour. The British losses had been more than two thousand, and they were almost a week burying them in the treacherous Louisiana mire during a truce granted for that purpose by Major General Andrew Jackson. Sir Edward Pakenham's body, however, was shipped back to England in a hogshead of rum, to preserve it.

The American losses were eight killed and thirteen wounded, and most of them were souvenir hunters who, against orders, had skipped out upon the stricken field to see what they could get—and were shot by dying redcoats who thought they were seeking scalps.

That was the battle of New Orleans.

6

WINNER TAKE NOTHING

That fracas on the plain of Chalmette abruptly changed a great many things.

It brought an end to Great Britain's plan to coop up the United States between the Atlantic Ocean and the Mississippi River. The occupation of New Orleans would have been a death grip on the whole of what was then the American interior, the Louisiana Purchase notwithstanding. Canada—loyal Canada!— nestled the new nation on the north; the British Navy, as it had just demonstrated, could easily close off the east and south; and the Mississippi, stoppered at New Orleans, held the whole of the west.

True, peace had already been agreed upon at Ghent, in Europe, at the time the battle of New Orleans was fought, but it had not been confirmed by either side, and the proposed treaty had not yet been ratified. If any man of that day, on either side of the sea, was so naive as to believe that England, having conquered the key to the American West, would gladly give it back to the loser because of what its envoys had initiated, such a person has left no record. The amusing suggestion that Great Britain had conquered half the world in a fit of absent-mindedness came later, and nobody has ever believed it anyway.

If the redcoats and Sutherlands had smashed that line at the Rodriguez Canal, the career of the United States as a possible world power would have met an untimely end right then and there, no matter how many diplomats drew up how many treaties in Belgium, and everybody knew it. Great Britain was not in the habit of returning loot.

The battle of New Orleans made a deep impression upon the American people, coming as it did at the end of an inglorious war. The American peace delegation had scored a brilliant triumph at Ghent, getting terms (though "Free Trade and Sailors' Rights" never were mentioned) much more advantageous than the United States government deserved, considering that when they were granted, the government was teetering on the edge of collapse. But a diplomatic victory is not exciting to the popular mind, not as thrilling as those casualty figures from Louisiana. Who was this man Jackson? people were asking. Military experts might point out, though in hushed voices, that he had done everything wrong. The fact remained that he had done one thing right—he had won. And how he had won! Something, obviously, must be done about him.

The Hero himself—he was always so spoken of, with a capital H—no doubt would have preferred to go home and see to the development of his freshly acquired acres, letting the honors fall where they would, but he had a strong sense of duty, and if his nation needed his services he could not withhold them.

Jackson had not pursued the British when they retreated across the cypress swamp and Lake Borgne, and the men who shifted pins in the big wall maps sadly but softly pronounced that as yet another mistake. However, after they had really gone, once and for all, he continued to act as governor of Louisiana for an unconscionably long time, while the Creoles fretted, impatient to get back to nonmilitary management. He had all sorts of disagreements with the civil authorities, whom he regarded as irksome gnats, and he declined all invitations to social affairs except those that were strictly in the line of duty. Therefore, the residents of the Crescent City, though they had hailed him on his return from the front and renamed their favorite square after him, in truth were glad at last to get rid of the General and to revert to their own easygoing administrators.

James Madison stepped down from the presidency, a tired man, and James Monroe, another of the Virginia Dynasty, took his place. One of the first things Monroe did was buy the Floridas, East and West, from Spain. He paid five million dollars. Andrew Jackson disapproved; he would simply have *taken* that territory. Indeed, he had offered to do as much when in the course of the Creek War he unhesitatingly invaded Florida in pursuit of some Indians who thought they could go on using the place as a refuge. "Let it be signified to me through any channel . . . that the possession of the Floridas would be desirable to the United States," he had written to Monroe, then Secretary of War, "and in sixty days it will be accomplished." Now it had been accomplished legally, without violence, and as though to give point to the matter, perhaps also to gain votes for the administration, the first governor-general to be named to the post was—Andrew Jackson.

He was given extraordinary powers, which he used badly. He didn't like Florida, nor did it like him. He brought Rachel with him, though he made it clear that he did not mean to stay long, but Rachel was only confused and saddened by the formal grandeur of queendom—for that is what it amounted to, so great was the new governor-general's power—and she soon made it clear that she would like to go back to Tennessee, to her own people.

The Hero quarreled noisily and needlessly with the functionaries of the departing government, and especially with the outgoing governor, a hidalgo with a very long name, whom his successor at one time actually put into jail. This shocked everybody, even the Hero's most ardent admirers, and it took all the diplomatic dexterity of the Secretary of State in Washington, the dour John Quincy Adams, to avert war.

In spite of that, Andrew Jackson, when at last he did go back to the Hermitage, was still the most loudly hailed man in the country, a national institution, a savior to be praised and even adored. His fame, no matter what he did or failed to do, seemed to grow. Already men were talking of him as a presidential possibility.

"I really hope you don't think that I'm damn fool enough to believe that," he cried to a friend, George Washington Campbell, who semiofficially sounded him out on the subject. "No, sir! I may be pretty well satisfied with myself in some things, but I am not vain enough for that!"

The talk persisted all the same.

The time was ripe for some such crashing change in our form of national government. The men who had framed the Constitution had not foreseen the emergence of political parties, which to them meant division, uncertainty, even chaos. Nevertheless, two parties had appeared early, and in the fourth presidential election of United States history, that of 1800, Thomas Jefferson's disputed and feared Republican Democrats had prevailed so emphatically over the "legitimate" party, the Federalists, that the Federalists, led or misled by Alexander Hamilton down the path of the right, of aristocracy, and of special privilege, had all but vanished. Since that time there had been for practical purposes but one political party, the Republican Democrats, or Democratic Republicans, and the men who controlled this party, largely congressmen and senators, were the men who nominated the man that the electorate, such as it was, would elect as President.

However, the electorate was being enlarged as states passed more liberal suffrage laws and immigrants with broad ideas poured in from Europe. Monroe was being a good chief executive, but it was generally understood that the Virginia dynasty was about to come to an end, and that new men, even a whole new class of men, might soon be voted into the White House. At the same time the congressional caucus system of national nominations was being looked upon with distaste, and men of the middle class, who until now had not been able to afford to take part in politics, were calling for something more democratic, more representative of the people as a whole.

So there might be something to this talk of the Hero of New Orleans as a presidential possibility, after all.

The field was open, the scramble horrendous. At the time that Jackson, in Nashville, was laughing at Judge Campbell's suggestion, observers in Washington pointed to no fewer than seventeen distinguished American men who, while they would not say it in so many words, needed only a feather's pressure to push them into candidacy.

The front-runner was William Harris Crawford of Georgia. He had everything, it seemed. He was large, handsome, hale, jovial, moderate in his views, a faithful follower of the Jeffersonian line. He had been Secretary of War and was now Secretary of the Treasury. He was acceptable to North and to South alike, and had been careful over the years to make no enemies. Most important, he had pledges of support from virtually all of the party leaders. Today he would be called the organization man, the machine choice. It was difficult to see how he could be prevented from winning the nomination.

But there was also Henry Clay. He was personally the most popular man in American politics. Homely, gay, with small twinkling gray eyes, the son of a Baptist minister but himself anything but parsonic of mien, he loved his liquor and his game of brag. Clay liked to play for high stakes. He was called the Mill Boy of the Slashes, also Harry of the West, and there was indeed something of young Lochinvar about him, although he was no regional candidate. He had devised or concocted something that he called the American System, which might have been regarded as suspiciously like the old Hamiltonian mercantilism if it had not been for the name, and this, featuring as it did high preferential tariffs, found acceptance in the North and East, especially among the ex-Federalists of New England.

There was John Quincy Adams, Monroe's Secretary of State, a Puritan with watery eyes, a rasping voice, and uncompromising crustiness. The gifted son of the second President of the United States, Adams was easily the best educated of the "possibles," and he had had more experience in foreign affairs than any of them.

There was John C. Calhoun, "the cast-iron man," of whom it was said that when he took snuff all South Carolina sneezed. He didn't take snuff often, though, and he never drank, gambled, or swore, and assuredly never cracked a joke. He was a somber man. He had black hair, a brow low but broad, a thin figure, and glorious bright yellow-brown eyes, but most of all he had an intellect. He was always thinking, which left no time for tears or laughter. He spoke loudly but carried a small stick.

There was the pouter-pigeon, polysyllabic Daniel Webster—"Black Dan" they used to call him at Dartmouth, so dark were his complexion and the color of his hair and eyes. He was the darling of the spectators' galleries, and everything he did and said was made to appear momentous and was accepted as such. If he so much as hiccupped he made it sound soul-shattering. He was probably the best lawyer in the country and certainly the highest paid. Though portentious, he drank, and now and then he would display a flash of grim, bitter humor. He always needed money, and had many rich friends.

There was Colonel Richard Mentor ("Rumpsey Dumpsey") Johnson, who like William H. Crawford had a deep booming voice and was strikingly handsome, and who like Andrew Jackson was a military hero. Johnson was a flamboyant figure, with a weakness for scarlet waistcoats. He had won the minor Battle of the Thames almost single-handedly, and in the course of it had himself slain the Indian leader, believed to be Tecumseh himself, thus giving his followers a catchy chant:

> Rumpsey Dumpsey,
> Rumpsey Dumpsey,
> Colonel Johnson
> Killed Tecumsey!

Johnson was well liked, and admired by many, but he had one insurmountable fault. He had been living with a Negro woman for years. This in itself would not have ruled him out, but Johnson the gallant wanted to marry her, and would have done so had it not been prohibited by Kentucky law, and he tried to get their two daughters accepted into respectable society.

There were other candidates, many others, although some began to fall off as the election year of 1824 approached.

All of these men feared the newcomer Andrew Jackson, whose name had been put into nomination by the Tennessee legislature, a move he had not initiated but certainly hadn't resisted either. He was something different, and the professionals did not know what to make of him.

There was no denying that thousands fairly worshipped this enigmatic man who remained silent on the other side of the mountain. Neither was there any denying the validity of his military fame, although many agreed with Henry Clay when he said that he could not believe "that killing two thousand five hundred Englishmen at New Orleans qualifies [a person] for the various, difficult, and complicated duties of the chief magistracy."

The political pond, never clear, became muddied to the point of impenetrability when, a good year and half before the election was due, Crawford, the favorite, took an overdose of lobelia for erysipelas and collapsed. For weeks, for months, they expected him to die at any minute. The great booming voice was reduced to a whisper, when he could make any sound at all. The breath came in jerks. The eyes were usually glazed. Nobody could be sure how much, if anything, he understood of what was said to him. He could not walk. Most of the time he could not even stir.

This had happened at the home of a friend in Virginia, a secluded estate, and Crawford's friends tried to keep it quiet. After all, this man, only fifty-one, still had in his pocket 114 of the 132 electoral votes needed to make him President. When, despite the rumors that were flying, they brought him back to Washington, they did so at night, and he lived in a house the shades of which were always drawn. Once, greatly daring, they took him for a ride in an open carriage, and he managed feebly to wave to a few friends. Later they took him to the Capitol, where they propped him in a chair in one of the committee rooms, and he greeted other friends, naming some by name, though in a small, weak voice, and shaking a few by hand. Yet the story persisted that he really was dead all this time.

The national party convention had not yet been born, but there were ways to nominate a man for the presidency besides the usual one of the congressional caucus, as the Tennessee legislature had learned. The caucus was held February 14, 1824, but only 68 of the 261 members of Congress took the trouble to attend. Of these, 64 voted for William Harris Crawford, who made no acceptance speech, being still in bed.

"Never before or since has there been such a formless, unorganized, chaotic and confusing presidential election" as that of 1824, says a respected authority.

By states, here is the way the electors voted that fall: three, with a total population of 1,212,337, for Clay; three, total population 1,497,029, for Crawford; seven, with 3,032,766, for Adams; eleven, population 3,757,756, for Andrew Jackson.

Jackson then was the winner of both the popular and the electoral votes, but as the Constitution stood then, since he did

71

not have a clear majority, the House of Representatives must decide among the top three. Clay was out. Calhoun had agreed to accept the vice presidency, no matter who won the big job. Crawford, moribund, saw his largest block of support, the New York delegation, under the leadership of natty little Martin Van Buren, preparing to switch to Jackson.

Some jumped to the conclusion that the Hero was as good as elected. Others, more wary, pointed out that Henry Clay, as Speaker, would be presiding over the special session of the House that would settle the matter. Clay, though famous as an orator—and these two accomplishments did not often go together—was even more famous as a parliamentarian. He knew Congress as nobody else ever had. Almost all of those who really counted owed him something, and these debts, carefully tabulated, he was prepared to produce at a moment's notice.

It snowed the day the House voted, a very dark day. The news too was dark, when at last it was announced. Henry Clay had prevailed. John Quincy Adams was elected.

Washington seethed—all the more excited because the Hero was in the city at the time. Would he accept this verdict? He was known to be an impetuous man, a man of flaming temper. Thousands throughout the country believed him to be their rightfully elected President and would go for their guns if Jackson only raised a hand. Would there be a revolution before morning?

They met, the winner and the loser, that very night at a formal reception. Jackson, a lady on each arm, approached John Quincy Adams, who was alone. Adams went pale. People fell away, silent, scared.

Jackson disengaged himself and bowed gracefully.

"Sir, my congratulations on your victory of this day."

Adams wetted his lips, nodding.

General Jackson offered his elbows to the ladies once more, and moved serenely away. Washington breathed again.

But that was not to be the end of it.

7

THE AGE OF ABUSE

The next morning, while he was packing for a return to Nashville, Andrew Jackson began to suspect that there might have been something irregular about that vote in the House of Representatives. Could it just be, he wondered, that Clay had arranged the slant in Adams's favor as a result of some previous promise? Was Harry of the West reaching for something, some office perhaps, that he could not otherwise expect to get? This thought troubled Jackson.

Friends, catching on, encouraged it. Wait and see, they cried. Pretty soon JQA will announce that Henry C. is to be the Secretary of State, and then we'll know that it was true, won't we?

The suspicion grew, throbbingly, poundingly, as these things will, like some bulging sore beneath the skin, as Jackson made his way, step by noisy step, back to Rachel and the Hermitage. He was not himself noisy on this trip—he spoke in public only when he had to, and then briefly and in a low voice—but those who greeted him at every stop showed less restraint, and again and again, hundreds of times a day, his hand was shaken while some wild-eyed citizen fervently assured him that he and not that stinking little squirt of an Easterner rightly ought to be the next President, that the election had been a crime, a theft. They believed this, and soon he did too.

Back at the Hermitage, his fears were confirmed when the

news came that President-elect Adams had indeed named Henry Clay Secretary of State, and that Clay had accepted. That, Jackson exclaimed, proved it! There had been a deal.

There had indeed, in all probability. There had been many deals before this one, and there have been many since, for the deal is an essential cog in the political machine, which cannot be run without it, and if it is usually quiet in its inception, it is only occasionally dirty or crooked. This one, surely, was innocent enough. Clay wanted the job and believed that he could handle it, and to get it, he was willing to use all his influence in the House of Representatives—an influence carefully cultivated over the years—not only to swing into the Adams camp all the congressmen personally pledged to him but also to twist the arms of many who had hitherto been uncommitted but who owed him, Henry Clay, favors.

Anyway, Clay believed that John Quincy Adams would be the better President.

Adams, for his part, undoubtedly believed that Henry Clay was the best man for State. These two had served together on the peace commission at Ghent, and though JQA had been shocked by Harry of the West's offstage behavior there—staying up all night, night after night, drinking and playing cards, for high stakes, too!—still he could not fail to perceive that Clay was the diplomat *par excellence.*

Andrew Jackson did not see it that way. To him the deal was nothing less than a betrayal of the American people. It was corruption at its worst. He said so again and again in letters to his well-wishers and friends, who had become legion.

These friends might be called the Jackson men, and they were something new in American politics. Many of them, perhaps most, had never even met the Hero, so they could hardly be said to have been carried away by his personality. Nor did they fall into line behind him because they admired his ideology. He had no ideology.

74

A man with a cause, especially a new cause, always attracts disciples if he shouts his beliefs loudly enough. But Jackson was a conservative rather than a reformer. There was a liberal movement afoot in Tennessee just then, led by William Carroll, but General Jackson had played no part in it. Nor was he likely to do so in the future. His friends and advisors were propertied men of the old school, who would instinctively oppose any innovation. He was no progressive. He considered himself, and was considered by all who knew him, an aristocrat.

It became increasingly clear, as 1828 loomed, that this would be a campaign not of issues—who cared for issues?—but of men. Not the glorification of candidates but their vilification would be its purpose.

There were sundry situations that should have been explained to the voters. There was, for instance, the preferential tariff. There had always been a tariff on imports—that was a part of Alexander Hamilton's original plan for funding the government. Hamilton, however, though fervently in favor of every device that would encourage the manufacturer, had proposed and put into effect a form of tariff that was designed for revenue only. He did not dream of a preferential tariff, a protective tariff, that would pick and choose among manufacturers, favoring now this one, now that, and raising prices generally, always at the expense of the farmer. Such a tariff was what Clay called for; it was an important part of his American System.

The new Jackson men, many of whom were newspaper publishers, did not brush off the Secretary of State as a mere background figure in the campaign of 1828, a person who, in the nature of his job, was President Adams's "man." Neither did they attack his plans for a high protective tariff as a permanent part of the government's policy, pointing out, as they might have done, that the heavy taxing of imported hemp at ports of entry might be related to the fact that hemp was the principal paying crop at Ashland, Clay's Kentucky plantation. Instead they concentrated on the man's private life, as they saw it. Thus, Isaac Hill in his *Concord* (New Hampshire) *Patriot* listed "Twenty-one Reasons Why Henry Clay Should Not Be Elected President," and No. 20 was "Because . . . he spends his days at the gaming table and his nights in a brothel."

The country was still predominantly rural—only one person out of fifteen lived in a town of eight thousand or over—and farmers could be expected to resent a high tariff. Yet as factories became more common in New England and the Middle Atlantic states, especially Pennsylvania, import taxes went up and up. The protective tariff was a divisive issue, exacerbating the regional feeling between North and South, and it was growing worse all the time. It should have been one of the chief issues in the election campaign of 1828, but it was barely mentioned.

A Virginian, John Randolph of Roanoke, said of the proposed tariff bill before the House of Representatives early in 1828 that it "refers to manufacturers of no sort or kind, except the manufacture of a President of the United States," and in the Senate it was a North Carolinian, William Drayton, who with a straight face proposed from the floor that the title of this bill be changed to "An act to increase the duties on certain imports for the purpose of increasing the profits of certain manufacturers." The formal title, however, was retained. The public called the thing the Tariff of Abominations.

As for the Hero himself, he would only say that he favored a "judicious" tariff.

The two administrations of James Monroe are known as the Era of Good Feeling. During that time, to all intents and purposes, only one political party existed in the United States, if Burke's definition of a party, the classic one, be accepted: "a body of men united for promoting by their joint endeavor the national interest upon some particular principle in which they are all agreed." That one party, however, like a bag blown up with too much hot air, was tugging at its tether and likely to split open. Of good feeling, therefore, very little could have been found. After the end of the Era, after the election of 1824, there was none.

Good feeling was certainly missing from the presidential campaign of 1828. Historians, who relish tags, have called this the Age of the Common Man. The Age of Abuse might be nearer the mark. Or the Age of Denigration.

The early Jackson men, the ones who rallied around him after 1824, could not be called common men. On the contrary, they were most uncommon. They were entering, for them, a new world, a world hitherto limited to those who had been born in the right places and who had gone to college. Neither were they common in the sense that they were not erudite or silken of manner. But they were "smart"; they were by no means fools or failures. Most of them were successful business or professional men who, having started with nothing, had made enough money to permit them to dabble in politics. They were thus model Americans. But common? No.

Some had joined Andrew Jackson because they found themselves for the first time in accord with a presidential candidate. More, it could be, joined him because they saw in him the coming man. As a later generation would put it, they jumped onto the bandwagon.

Whatever their reasons, they were an extraordinary lot, America's first "practical politicians." The phrase was not pejorative then, as it is now. Why shouldn't a politician be practical? Would you want the government to be run by impractical persons?

The most remarkable of these new men who were to set the political pace was Martin Van Buren. Typical of them he could not be called, for he was not typical of anything; he was unique. He came from Old Kinderhook, New York, and although he was a lawyer he had had no more schooling than Andrew Jackson, for his parents were poor and the family a large one.

ANDREW JACKSON, HERO

His rise in politics had been meteoric, but you would never have guessed it, to see him. He was small, quiet-spoken, soft-footed, and had fleecy red side-whiskers. He favored, in daytime, snuff-colored coats, white trousers, lace-tipped cravats, yellow gloves, and morocco shoes. In wet weather he might wear spats. He carried a gold-headed cane. He was fussy about his food, choosy with wines. He orated well enough, though he never thought that he was God and neither did the ladies in the gallery; nothing memorable survives from his speeches.

Many men hated Martin Van Buren, though they could not have said why. It must have been mostly a matter of jealousy. He always seemed to get things done his way. He was forever pulling rabbits out of a hat. And they were good rabbits, and the hat too was a good one, nobby, made of the very best beaver. The politics of New York were labyrinthine, even downright Byzantine, but Marty Van was scarcely out of his teens when he was leading them in every detail, cracking his whip like the ringmaster in a circus, though never raising his voice. He was the head of what was then called the Albany Regency; today it would be called the state machine. He was also, at the time of Andrew Jackson's emergence upon the national political scene, a United States senator.

A tireless worker, Van Buren possessed an unrivaled talent for holding his tongue, and when accused of some heinous political crime, as so often he was, he would open wide with reproach his big, baby-blue, baby-innocent eyes, but he would say nothing. As a modern historian (who doesn't like him) puts it, Martin Van Buren "seldom committed himself and then only in terms as equivocal and disarming as possible. He was a lamb who led lions." As the caustic John Randolph (who did like him) put it, "He rowed to his object with muffled oars."

He was called the Little Magician, the American Talleyrand, the Red Fox of Kinderhook, and sometimes Sweet Sandy Whiskers. It was said of him that he used French perfume, that he put coon oil in his hair, even that he wore corsets. He smiled mildly at these accusations, and walked on. No mud ever stuck to him.

He was not, in fact, a Merlin. He could choose wrong, though he never chose hastily. As long as William H. Crawford was alive and willing to let his name be used, Martin Van Buren stayed with him, as per previous agreement. Once the election of 1824 was over and Crawford was clearly out of the presidential race (he did recover sufficiently to accept a judgeship of the northern circuit in Georgia, where he served until his death September 15, 1834), Martin Van Buren did not need to survey the rest of the field. He already had picked his man. He offered his services to Andrew Jackson.

Thereafter and for the rest of the Hero's life Marty Van was the political manager of the Jackson movement. It is unlikely, though, that he ever participated in the smears. He was a kindly man, naturally polite, a fastidious man who would have found no pleasure slobbering in slime. Also, public relations was not his metier, and neither was journalism, and he was no adventurer to break a path into unfamiliar fields. Yet, like the Hero himself, he did not feel called upon to gainsay the lies when printed or to forbid the publication of new ones, howsoever horrid. He did not think that a part of his duty.

Crawford, then, was out of the race. Clay, who might well have preferred being right to being President*, but had no unalterable objection to being both, likewise could not be consid-

*Authorities differ as to the origin of Henry Clay's most famous statement. H. L. Mencken in his New Dictionary of Quotations has it as part of a speech in the Senate in 1850: "Sir, I would rather be right than be President." But the Oxford Dictionary of Quotations has it: "I had rather be right than President," and says it was used in a letter to Senator Preston of South Carolina in 1839. Bartlett agrees with Mencken, Stevenson (Home Book of Quotations) with the Oxford. A contemporary commentator, William Safire, in his The New Language of Politics (Macmillan, 1972), thinks that it might be both.

ered an active candidate, because of his peculiar relationship to President Adams. At one time early in the campaign of 1824 there was some talk of a ticket headed by JQA with Jackson in the second spot as a candidate for the vice presidency, so that a few of the boys had even started to practice a marching chant:

> John Quincy Adams,
> Who can write.
> And Andrew Jackson,
> Who can fight.

Nothing came of this preposterous suggestion, and it was not even mentioned in the 1828 campaign. John C. Calhoun would remain vice president. He did not enjoy the post, which allowed little room for him to exercise his intellect, but people still generally believed that either the Vice President or the Secretary of State would become the next president, so the "cast-iron man" settled back with a sigh to wait out another four years.

It would be Adams versus Jackson. There was no doubt about that.

Adams had been a good President, a very careful one. It was hard to find anything in the record to attack him on. His private life was shamelessly blameless, for he was the most vinegarish prude imaginable.

JQA's wife Louisa was English, but attempts to circulate stories to the effect that she was a British spy who had striven to soften his attitude toward the enemy in the War of 1812 failed when less excitable Jackson men pointed out that the Adamses had not been in the United States during that conflict: they had been in Germany or Russia, where he was an ambassador.

A more telling accusation was that of profligate gaming

in the White House. A billiard table, playing cards, even pairs of dice, the papers implied, had all been installed since the occupancy of John Quincy Adams—installed, they also hinted, at public expense. The President, who probably would have fainted at the sight of a deck of cards in his own home, and wouldn't have known what dice were, did quaveringly admit that he liked a solo game of billiards now and then. Together with an occasional nude swim in some remote part of the Potomac, billiards was his only sports indulgence—but he hastened to add that the table and cues and balls at the Executive Mansion had not been paid for by the United States government. They had been a gift to him, the President, by his son, who paid for them out of his own pocket.

At one time Jacksonian journalists actually accused John Quincy Adams of being a Unitarian, but this charge too fell flat. The people of New England simply would not believe such a thing of an Adams, whereas outside of New England nobody knew what a Unitarian was anyway.

These extraordinary tales originated in the Washington *Globe*, a paper owned and edited by Duff Green, one of the earliest of the Jackson men, although personally he was attached to his father-in-law, John C. Calhoun. The *Globe*'s motto was "The World Is Governed Too Much."

It was Isaac Hill of New Hampshire, a small cadaverous man, who set off the most astounding anti-Adams explosion. He did this not in his newspaper, the *Patriot*, but in a campaign biography, *Brief Sketch of the Life, Character and Services of Major General Andrew Jackson*, which he published just before the election, leaving no time for effective refutation. It was the first time that this particular trick was used, though it was to become an accepted part of the American political scene after the presidential campaign of 1844, when a pseudonymous travel writer, Baron von Roorbach, published a last-minute book in which he described a mistreated coffle of slaves who belonged to one of the candidates, James K. Polk. The device thereupon became known—and still is—as a roorbach. Polk won the election anyway.

Hill gravely announced in his biography of Jackson that John Quincy Adams had once been a pimp.

Ambassador Adams, he said, had arranged for an affair between Czar Alexander I and a female member of his own household, one Martha Godfrey, nurse to his son Charles Francis Adams, then a tot. This was supposed to have happened in Russia, years before.

The President answered this charge promptly. There had been a Martha Godfrey, yes; she was now happily married and living in Boston. The Czar had indeed expressed a wish to meet her, though not for any carnal purpose, and the ambassador had arranged such a meeting. It had come to nothing because the Czar had very little English, which he spoke with such a heavy German accent that Miss Godfrey couldn't make it out, while she had no other language than English, which she spoke through her nose, like a good Yankee. The interview, in any event, had lasted only about three minutes, at midday, in one of the public rooms of the palace, and John Quincy Adams himself was right there all the time, so we can be sure that there was no copulation.

Nothing indicates that Andrew Jackson ever had anything to do with the concoction of these clumsy scandals, but neither is there anything to indicate that he ever lifted a finger to check them.

Jackson's enemies concentrated upon his temper, his harshness, his ambition. They rekindled in the voters, again and again, their traditional fear of professional soldiers, of militarism. Their most extreme argument—as it was probably the most effective, too—was in the form of the famous "Coffin Hand Bill," the inspiration of a Philadelphia newspaperman. This bill, which proclaimed Andrew Jackson to be a murderer because he had caused six would-be deserters in the Creek War to be shot, was decorated with the likenesses of six black coffins. Actually, at one time or other General Jackson had ordered and seen carried out no fewer than eleven military executions, but these six, being in one batch, all of them scared, bewildered youngsters, seemed especially deplorable.

Jacksonites countered this with a paid advertisement:

Cool and Deliberate Murder.—Jackson cooly and deliberately put to death upward of fifteen hundred British troops on the 8th of January, 1815, on the plains below New Orleans, for no other offense than that they wished to sup in the city that night.

The practical politicians' invariable retort to any charge of militarism was: Well, he won, didn't he? It was unanswerable. Andrew Jackson, after all these years, was still the Hero, the most admired American since George Washington. Military tyranny, pooh! This man was "the conqueror of the conquerors of Bonaparte." What more could you ask?

Out of the welter of lies and insults, now on this side, now on that, the unkindest cut of all was one of the last. It was aimed at the Jackson women, mother and wife, the one long dead, the other dying. Mrs. Andrew Jackson, Sr., the emigrant from Ireland, had died of a disease contracted when she worked among war prisoners as an unpaid volunteer nurse, but now, at the very tail of this disgraceful campaign, an Adams journal announced that once upon a time she had been a prostitute. That there wasn't a grain of truth in the statement made no difference. There was no time for a denial anyway. As for Rachel, she died before she could know that her husband had been elected President of the United States but not before she could know that the papers were calling her an adultress.

Then the returns came in. There were 261 electoral votes. It would require 131 of these to constitute a majority. Jackson got 178, John Quincy Adams 83. The popular vote (omitting

South Carolina and Delaware, the only states that still elected electors by legislature) was 647,276 for Jackson, 508,064 for Adams.

Here was a clear-cut victory, leaving nothing to be compromised or modified, and the practical politicians were jubilant. It was with a heavy heart, however, that Andrew Jackson, now a widower, prepared to go back to Washington.

.

8

PEOPLE WILL TALK

Jackson's administration could be said to have started not with a bang but with a giggle.

He was immersed in the almost unbelievably complex anfractuosities of cabinet-making, upstairs at the Indian Queen, where he had barricaded himself against job-seekers, when, late in the year, John Henry Eaton came calling. He at least was not looking for a job. Or was he?

Major Eaton, barely twenty-nine, had been elected to the United States Senate, its youngest member and by all odds its handsomest. He was the catch of the season—a widower, amiable, very rich. He came from Tennessee, the President-elect's own state.

"Sir, I want to marry Peggy O'Neale. Do you think I should? You know what people are saying."

Yes, the President-elect knew what people were saying. He lighted his pipe, a large thing with a wooden stem and a red clay bowl known as a Powhatan, and he nodded to Senator Eaton to sit down. Yes, they were saying that these two had been carrying on secretly, even before Peggy's husband had died on the other side of the sea.

Peggy was the daughter of William and Rhoda O'Neale, who for a long time ran the Franklin House, one of the best inns in Washington. A green-eyed brunette with a ready laugh,

Peg was a favorite of the customers, largely male, who bounced her on their knees as long as it was decent to do so. Precocious, she drew their drinks, and she sometimes danced for them, for she was a very good dancer, who at the age of thirteen had won a prize handed to her by that aging but still vivacious Juno, Dolley Madison, former First Lady of the Land. Everybody knew Peggy O'Neale. She had always had charm, and as she grew up it developed that she had a fine figure as well.

"The smartest little woman in America, yes, sir," Senator Andrew Jackson had called her, more than once. He had said it with respect, and in this he differed from Henry Clay, another habitué of the Franklin House, who in discussing Peggy over a bottle one night cried, "No! Age cannot wither nor custom stale her infinite virginity."

This girl, it must be admitted, did little to refute the rumors. The very name, Peggy O'Neale, suggested a saucy barmaid who might be as free with her physical charms as she was with her language, having been brought up among roisterers. She sang readily enough, she danced, she rolled her eyes, and there was little wonder that, men being men, she came to seem accessible.

There was a young congressman from Tennessee, who, like the most distinguished member of his state's delegation, Andrew Jackson, was staying at the Franklin House. He was deeply in love with his young wife back home, but he was lonesome, and when he came back from the Capitol one afternoon after a hard session of debate he seized upon this luscious waitress— and was astounded by her resistance. The congressman persisted, attempting to brush aside what could only be conventional coyness, and Peg had to hit him with the snatched-up fire tongs. Hurt, he appealed to General Jackson, who told him that he'd got what he deserved and asked him why he had assumed that Peggy O'Neale would go to bed with him.

The congressman simply couldn't understand. "Everybody at the bar said she would," he cried. The bar he meant was the one at the Capitol, where our lawmakers often discussed such matters.

Peg had no aversion to marriage as such. She was barely fifteen when she tried to elope in the dead of night with a young army officer, a guest at the hotel, but her alert father prevented it. Like her mother, he was hoping that Peg would make a brilliant match. She did not. When a few years later, in the middle of June, 1816, she tied herself to John Bowie Timberlake, the union was not a promising one.

Timberlake was a purser in the U.S. Navy, not even an officer. He drank, but he was a quiet drinker, not quarrelsome, though never gay either. He was a bore. Moreover, he habitually had trouble with his accounts. Nobody accused Timberlake of stealing money, but undoubtedly arithmetic was not his forte, and when at the end of a voyage the purser's books still didn't balance he was in effect suspended. Technically he was a civilian, though subject to naval discipline, and the navy could sue him for the money that was missing. He was desperate. By that time he had had two children by Peggy, still no more than a girl, and the marriage, though unexciting, seemed firm. What to do?

Senator Eaton came along at this point. Whether he lent Timberlake money without security, or gave him money, or whether he made an undercover deal with the navy's accounting department, we will never know. At any rate, Timberlake was released from what had amounted to house arrest and was assigned to another ship, one that was about to go on a long voyage.

He never returned from that voyage. The official report had him dying in a Mediterranean port on April 2, 1828, of "a pulmonary disease." But Washington society would not be satisfied with that. Rumor immediately had it that Timberlake, in a mood of despondency brought about by brooding over his wife's affair with the young senator from Tennessee, and while drunk, of course, had cut his own throat.

So the former Peggy O'Neale was a *femme fatale*, Washington's first, and the capital cackled in delight.

The President-elect knew all this. He put his Powhatan into an ash receiver and dismissed the caller with a nod. "Well, if you love her why don't you marry her, and shut their mouths?"

Then he went back to the business of selecting secretaries.

It was an arduous business. The age had a much higher regard for members of the executive council than we do today, though it is hard to see why. There is no provision in the Constitution for a cabinet, and Washington throughout his two administrations never even used the word, referring rather to "the heads of departments." There were only four of them at first—State, War, Treasury, and Attorney General. The Department of the Navy had not yet been created, the Postmaster General was a bureaucrat who did not aspire to ministerial rank, and it would be a long time before the Vice President was considered a member of the cabinet. Washington used to put large matters before them, usually as questions, and then listen while they talked about them, deciding at last in favor of the majority, or, if they split evenly, as they usually did, in favor of his own original belief.

The second President, John Adams, had kept these men on, not because he liked them—he didn't, and by and large they didn't like him—but because in the absence of any directions in the Constitution he conceived it to be his duty. Most of them, the strongest ones, were under the thumb of the first Secretary of the Treasury, Alexander Hamilton, now in private law practice with an office in Wall Street, New York City. They reported everything to Hamilton, and received instructions from him, without telling their nominal boss, President Adams. When the President learned about this he exploded in rage, firing cabinet secretaries right and left, an act that Hamilton took as a personal affront.

All this split the Federalist party right down the middle,

permitting Thomas Jefferson and his liberals to slip into power. Jefferson and the two Virginians who followed him into the White House, Madison and Monroe, treated *their* secretaries with dignity but not much confidence, and the New Englander who became the sixth President, John Quincy Adams, did the same.

One might suppose, then, that by the time Andrew Jackson's star rose in the West the cabinet would no longer be looked upon with awe, nor its formation be esteemed a momentous act. The very opposite was true. The cabinet, under the Hero, would become, it was believed, all-important. As in England, it would *be* the government.

The reasons for this belief were personal, as everything that touched General Jackson was personal. There were those who hated him and those who loved him, the latter being a majority. Those who hated him feared him, of course, and they feared for the nation under his command. In their eyes he was, or was about to become, a despot; he was bigoted, arrogant, ambitious, irresponsible, and hence, more than any president who had gone before him, he needed the help of able men, experienced men, statesmen, who would steer him and restrain him. Even those who loved the President-elect took little stock in his ability to conduct affairs of state. They questioned not only his sagacity but his taste, indeed his very sense. He was grand; unquestionably in the long run he would be good for the country; but unquestionably too he was ignorant, and he needed advice, guidance.

Both sides, agreeing at least in this, thought that the greatest danger that faced the country, under what would surely be a new and different kind of administration, was the emergence of that old Anglo-Saxon devil, a royal favorite. If a villain got the ear of this simple soldier, they feared, the structure of the United States government might be razed to its foundation. Ergo, there must be appointed a sane, very strong, and intelligent cabinet. The Hero must be protected against himself.

The task would have been knotty at best, but with all this protective pressure being brought to bear upon him, from right as well as from left, the President-elect, a man accustomed to making his own decisions, for a time was fairly overwhelmed. He worked hard at it. He received and listened to all of the friends of friends who had candidates to urge upon him. He made notes. He consulted maps. He checked records. At last he came up with a slate.

State, Martin Van Buren; Treasury, Samuel D. Ingham of Pennsylvania; War, Senator Eaton; Postmaster General, William T. Barry; Navy, John Branch, North Carolina; Attorney General, John M. Berrien, Georgia.

A howl of rage arose. Nobody liked the list. "The most unintellectual cabinet we ever had," avowed a noted ex-Federalist, a man who believed that anybody who couldn't read Thucydides in the original was a red-necked barbarian. But his description was applauded. At this time, too, and because of the first Jackson cabinet, the phrase coined by some anonymous newspaperman, "the millennium of the minnows," came to be applied to the Jackson era.

What was so bad about this cabinet? Had the experts expected angels? Each man appointed was a reputable and even praiseworthy citizen of the United States. Geography, too, had been taken into consideration. Virginia had not been kowtowed to, nor had New York, despite Van Buren, who, as it turned out, was the one member of the cabinet everyone had expected to be there. Ingham was from Pennsylvania, Barry from Kentucky, Branch and Berrien from the Old South. The President-elect had not favored Tennesseans, as many feared that he might: there was only Senator Eaton. The real trouble was that this slate did not answer the question of who was going to be the *next* President of the United States, the *post-Jackson* President.

Andrew Jackson had announced that he sought one term

only and would not stand to be reelected. All American history, so far, had shown that a President should first have been a Vice President or else Secretary of State—often, though not of course at the same time, both. John Adams, Thomas Jefferson, James Madison, James Monroe, and John Quincy Adams had maintained this tradition. And the present slate—although no one would admit it in public—was *too* fair. John Caldwell Calhoun was Vice President, yes, but Martin Van Buren was to be Secretary of State. Barry was a Marty Van man, and so Eaton would be if the Hero whistled. Berrien and Branch were for Calhoun. Unintellectual?

One thing at least was certain: however capable and even admirable each of these men might be by himself, they were not accordant. Branch and Van Buren would not even speak to one another; the Southerners distrusted the Secretary of State because he threatened the rise of their god, Calhoun; Ingham, a straightlaced Bucks County Quaker, looked with vinegarish disapproval upon the easygoing ways of amiable Willy Barry.

These were not men (Van Buren excepted) whom the new President would have picked as his advisors of his own volition. They were named for political reasons, as cabinet members customarily are, but Americans, who had not yet learned to accept this necessity, and who still feared the appearance of that sinister figure the favorite, clucked their tongues and shook their heads when the names were recited.

This doubt did not dismay the Hero, who indeed might have been unaware of it. As a general in the field he had seldom called a council of war, and so now, as President, he seldom called a meeting of the cabinet. When he did, it was not to formulate policy but only to comment on the progress of the government and to hear reports on the welfare of the various departments. No favorite, male or female, would have found a place there.

In public a ramrod, the President was formality itself when

some ceremony had to be performed, and his dinners, many and sumptuous, were exceedingly proper and invariably graced by his own presence, though often he was too ill to eat. When it came to soliciting advice, that was a different matter. Rigidity no longer reigned. He would send a messenger to summon this friend or that, one perhaps in the government, perhaps not, and this personage soon would come calling. Unannounced, he would go up to the second floor of the White House, and without knocking or even calling out he would enter the President's pipe-smelly study, a room stacked to the ceiling with work. No record was made of these meetings.

There was Major William B. Lewis, "the great father of the wire-pullers," tall, broad-shouldered, with an open manner and a booming voice. He served as a sort of appointments secretary, living in the White House. He watched Congress. He was tireless and tirelessly loyal, a slave.

There was Duff Green, a brilliant newspaperman, still young, seemingly sage, but thought by many to be a White House spy for his father-in-law, Vice President Calhoun.

There was Roger B. Taney (pronounced *Tawny*), a sardonic lawyer from Maryland, a dedicated Jeffersonian, who loved to smoke long black cigars. (He was to go down in history as the Supreme Court chief justice who promulgated the Dred Scott decision.)

There was Francis P. Blair (*Bla-ar* to the President), another editor, small and mousy, with a mind like a whip, who was to build a famous Washington house.

There was Isaac Hill of New Hampshire, who limped and leered, and whose editorials could only be called excoriating. He was the most hated man in Washington, for he never cared whom he insulted. He was poor, and to keep him around the place the President nominated him for second controller of the treasury, a nomination the antiadministration forces in the Senate managed to kill. Hill, however, needed to go home only long enough to get himself elected to the U.S. Senate, and when he entered that famous chamber it was as one of its members. There was Felix Grundy, stocky, dark, beetle-browed, another newspaperman.

There was Amos ("The Deacon") Kendall, a Dartmouth graduate, small, wizened, prematurely gray—his hair was white by the time he was forty-five—who almost never said anything to anybody except the Chief himself. "Wily" was the word most often used to describe him. Legends sprang up about his Machiavellianism. He was even compared with that political magician, Martin Van Buren, the only member of this group of small, young, acerbic followers of the President who also was a member of the cabinet.

Even Marty Van failed to fill the role of the baleful favorite, though of the lot he was closest to the throne. He and Jackson used to go riding almost every morning on the Tenallytown Road, a sight to see, one tall, one small, in earnest talk.

These advisors were called, collectively, the Kitchen Cabinet, but the name was misleading. There was nothing sneaky about them. Their ability was marked, their devotion to Andrew Jackson touching. They had all been successful business or professional men before they got into politics, lawyers or newspaper editors or both, who instinctively shunned the limelight. No President before this had been and probably none since has been so well served by unselfish friends.

All, then, seemed well. But it wasn't. The Kitchen Cabinet, which never did meet as a body, functioned smoothly enough, but the same could not be said of the conventional, the "official" cabinet, the one the public saw.

Peggy Timberlake, née O'Neale, and young Senator John Henry Eaton, who was about to become Secretary of War, took the advice of the President-elect. They got married the night of January 1, 1829, and spent their honeymoon in, of all places, Philadelphia. It was when they returned to Washington that the trouble started.

9

DID THE LADY
OR DIDN'T SHE?

John C. Calhoun, "the cast-iron man," was noted chiefly for his intellect. Nobody ever mentioned him without referring to it or at least having it in mind. He was noted too for his oratory. His words, whether in the Senate chamber or in private quarters, boomed and bounced back and forth like echoes in a cave, reverberating with profound thoughts. He was not, however, remarkable for his ability to listen. He loved an audience but did not care for company. "There is no *relaxation* with him," Senator Dixon of Alabama (who weighed 430 pounds) complained. When you talked to him he ordinarily kept his mouth shut and looked at you, but you knew that he wasn't heeding a word; you could see that he was only rehearsing what *he* would say as soon as he got a chance, if not sooner.

Harriet Martineau, the redoubtable English novelist who visited America at this time, carried a huge ear trumpet, which was disconcerting for the personages she interviewed, but she had a habit of getting things straight, and she knew how to express herself on paper. Calhoun and his celebrated brain fascinated her, and she was to set down her impression of him in her best-selling *Society in America.*

It is at first extremely interesting to hear Mr. Calhoun talk, and there is a never-failing evidence of power in all he says and does which commands intellectual reverence; but the admiration is too soon turned into regret, into absolute melancholy. It is impossible to resist the conviction that all this force can be at best but useless, and it is but too likely to be very mischievous. His mind has long lost all power of communicating with any other. I know of no man who lives in such utter intellectual solitude. He meets men, and harangues them by the fireside as in the Senate; he is wrought like a piece of machinery, set going vehemently by a weight, and stops while you answer; he either passes by what you say, or twists it into a suitability with what is in his head, and begins to lecture again.

In the South Carolina of that time you were nothing if you were not a gentleman, and a gentleman was a person who owned many slaves and acres. Calhoun's intellect counted for him only after he had been accepted as such by his fellow Carolinians. He had not inherited the acres and slaves that gained him admittance into the ranks of the blessed; neither had he earned them by the sweat of his brow; he had married them.

His very education, concededly a good one—Yale and then the prestigious law school at Litchfield, Connecticut—had been paid for by a rich cousin, Floride Calhoun, and when the young statesman after much searching of his soul consented to marry this lady's daughter, also named Floride, the widow, Floride *mère,* handsomely endowed Floride *fille* for the occasion, which was how John C. Calhoun came to be elevated to the gentry. These two young persons got along very well—they had fourteen children—and in most matters Floride *fille* was a dutiful and respectful wife, although now and then she would put her foot down, and John C. Calhoun perforce would listen.

Floride put her foot down when the Eatons, the newlyweds, returned from Philadelphia. The new Washington season was about to begin, she pointed out, and if he, John, for one moment thought that she, Floride, had any intention of receiving or being received by That Woman, he was out of his mind.

The situation became even more acute, became indeed impossible, when the wives of three cabinet secretaries, Berrien,

Branch, and Ingham, all Calhoun followers, announced that they agreed with Floride.

This state of affairs was somewhat more than a tempest in a teapot. It was a scandal of the first magnitude, and as soon as the public outside Washington heard about it, it could at the very outset of this new, controversial, democratic Era of the Common Man bring the gears of government to a halt.

The President made the matter even worse when he cried, "She is as pure as the undriven snow!" and donned his bright armor and mounted his white horse and galloped off to the relief of beauty in distress.

Incidents occurred, and there would be more. When, at a formal dinner, the wife of the Dutch ambassador, Madame de Bangeman Huygens, learned that she was about to be seated next to the Aspasia of Washington—or, as some called her, since she was the wife of the Secretary of War, Bellona—she called for her husband's arm and ostentatiously took her leave. Jackson was not present, but when he heard about it the next morning he blew up. He would have demanded an apology or even demanded of the government of the Netherlands that it recall Huygens, had not Martin Van Buren talked him out of it.

Marty Van's parents in upper New York State had brought him up speaking Dutch at home, and he liked to remember it and practice it with the Huygenses, as he liked to drink their Schiedam. The Secretary of State in fact was a favorite among the diplomatic set, and not just because of his office. He kept several of that set away from seizure by the "Eaton Malaria," and one, the British ambassador, he definitely enlisted on the President's side, persuading him to give a "squeezy" party in honor of Peg. Van Buren did the same with Baron Krudenwe, a Russian, the only other bachelor (besides Sir Leslie Vaughan) in the diplomatic corps.

Marty, dapper little Marty Van, indeed was a tower of strength to the President in this unfortunate, this woefully hysterical affair. A widower of many years' standing, he had three strapping sons but no daughter, and so he was free to give his arm to the disputed beauty any time he liked, no matter how formal the function, as he was free to use his own judgment in the matter of accepting or rejecting invitations. His help at the White House was appreciated, and he quickly became a sort of administration master of ceremonies, the arbiter of all things social in Washington, except for Floride Calhoun and her friends.

A political purpose was assigned to this, of course. Everything that Sweet Sandy Whiskers did was believed to have a political motive, and if a motive could seldom be found, well, that was all the more reason to exclaim upon the subtlety of the fellow.

It could be, as some men said, that the Secretary of State performed these favors only to please the President and by contrast displease the Vice President, his rival for the succession. More likely he did them out of the kindness of his heart. He had always been a thoughtful man, attentive to the needs of the lonesome, the timorous, the unskilled.

Nevertheless Floride stood firm, and so did her friends.

Jackson seethed. The slanders against Peggy Eaton were mixed in his mind, somehow, with the slanders against his own dear Rachel, and resentment found tinder for its spark in this lonely man. When the clergymen began to lob letters at him he almost exploded.

He had always been respectful toward wearers of the cloth, but though a believer in God, he had subscribed to no church until late in life when Rachel, after many years of effort, persuaded him to become a Presbyterian. Their minister in Washington while the Hero was a senator was the Reverend J. N. Campbell, and when the President-elect returned to the capital, he more or less kept up the connection, though Rachel was no longer alive. Yet he was to learn, to his amazement, that

97

it was from the Reverend J. N. Campbell that most of the vilification came.

Campbell wrote to a fellow divine, the Reverend Ezra Stiles Ely, rector of a fashionable Philadelphia church and an old acquaintance of Andrew Jackson, who had recently been in Washington to witness the inauguration. The writer confessed that he hesitated to take up so delicate a matter with his distinguished parishioner, and asked Ely if *he* wouldn't do so. The Reverend Mr. Ely responded eagerly and instantly. He wrote a long personal letter to Andrew Jackson, who had barely finished his unpacking at the Executive Mansion.

Jackson wrote an even longer reply, denying everything. The lady, he cried yet again, was as pure as any angel. He should know. He, a senator then, had been rooming with Major Eaton in the same building with Purser and Mrs. Timberlake at the time when Peg and Major Eaton were supposed to be having their amour, and he could assure the padre that they simply didn't have time for such a thing. He had been present—as had Senator Eaton—when Mrs. Timberlake and her two children said farewell to Timberlake at the beginning of that long Mediterranean cruise from which the purser was never to return, and a happier, more contented couple, he averred, you could not have found. This letter, very long, was not dictated. It was respectful, but exceedingly firm.

The Reverend Mr. Ely wrote to the Reverend Mr. Campbell in Washington, and Campbell wrote back, reavowing Peg's guilt and supplying a few more details, including a trip to New York that Peggy and Senator Eaton were said to have taken while Timberlake was away. They had stayed overnight in a hotel, Campbell related, and had registered as man and wife.

The Reverend Mr. Ely forwarded this information, in another long letter, to the President.

Jackson replied at even greater length, still respectful but this time with a slight edge of asperity. He answered—decisively, it would seem—one of Ely's chief charges, that the newlyweds, some time before they were married, had spent a night together in a New York hotel. He, the President of the United States, had engaged an investigator to go to New York and check the hotel's register—in vain. He had paid this private eye out of his own pocket.

The letter seems to have impressed Ely, who then wrote to Campbell suggesting that he call upon the President in person. This Campbell did, on September 1, 1829. It was the first time Jackson learned that his own minister was behind the business. He called in a couple of witnesses, just to be sure that the record was kept, and when the interview was over he wrote a long and careful account of it, an account you may read today in the Jackson papers at the Library of Congress, for it has been retained as an official document.

To the man of God, Andrew Jackson proved, immediately and conclusively, that the charge of a night in a New York hotel was false. He went from there to another Ely charge—though this too, it now developed, had come originally from Campbell—that Peggy Timberlake at a time when her husband had been at sea for almost a year had had a miscarriage. The assumption of course was that Major Eaton was responsible for it. The story rested, in the first place, on the reputed testimony of a Dr. Craven, a physician who had been called in to attend Peg but had arrived too late. This Dr. Craven was now dead, and he had left no written account of the alleged miscarriage he didn't claim to have witnessed anyway.

When had this happened? the President demanded. In 1826, the pastor replied. But all through 1826, the President triumphantly cried, Purser Timberlake, who was in trouble with the navy about his accounts, was ashore, reporting regularly, as the records would show, and living with his wife. Campbell then shifted his ground. No, he remembered now, it was not 1826 but 1821. After several hours of this, the President sent him away.

The President still did not think that Peg Eaton had been

fully cleared, so he summoned both Ely and Campbell to attend him at the White House the evening of September 10, and directed all members of his cabinet—the real cabinet, not the Kitchen Cabinet—to be there.

We have no official record of this meeting. We do know that the Reverend J. N. Campbell brought his lawyer with him, a part-time poet from Baltimore, Francis Scott Key.

No lawyer, no matter how lyrical, was going to avert the wrath of the Hero. The White House aides could have foretold as much. The aides knew that the President, even this early in his administration, sometimes faked a fit of rage, raising his left fist and swearing "by the ee-TARN-al!" his favorite oath, when he sought to get rid of some tiresome delegation. His tantrums were notorious, and this oath never failed to scare the visitors away. Afterward President Jackson would collapse into an armchair, chuckling, and reach for one of his pipes. However, the aides had come to know when the Hero truly was angry, when a real storm was about to break. On such occasions, in advance, the left side of the President's mouth used to twitch upward.

The left side of his mouth was twitching when he greeted the visitors on September 10. The cabinet secretaries noticed it too.

The Reverend Mr. Campbell had been doing some investigating of his own, and now, perhaps heartened by the presence of his lawyer, he confessed that Purser Timberlake had not been at sea throughout 1826, when the miscarriage was supposed to have occurred. It was 1821, he said again. He was sure of it.

The President, excited, shook a fist. This Dr. Craven, whoever he was, had been summoned, too late, to the scene of a miscarriage—in 1826, wasn't that right? Yes!

The Reverend Mr. Campbell demurred. What he had said at first was 1826, but what he had *meant,* really, was 1821. Now, if he was permitted to explain . . .

He had been brought there to give evidence, not to interpret it, he was told. And by the ee-TARN-al . . .

The Reverend Mr. Campbell wrapped his dignity about him like a clerical coat. If he was not to be allowed to explain, he said, obviously his usefulness there was at an end. He begged leave to leave.

Admirably upright, he went out. He was followed by his lawyer, and a little later by the Reverend Mr. Ely, who had not said a word. Soon after this the President dismissed the cabinet.

Andrew Jackson appeared to believe that this curious meeting closed the incident and that Peggy O'Neale Timberlake Eaton, ex-barmaid, had now been fully exonerated. He was mistaken. Floride Calhoun stayed firm. She still had no intention of attending any party, she said, of which That Woman would be a member. And Mrs. Ingham and Mrs. Branch and Mrs. Berrien agreed.

Here was a split, right down the middle, of the new administration. It was not yet public property, but it soon would be, and how, then, could the President operate?

The sting of the thing came home to him, literally, when Emily Donelson, the White House hostess, the acting First Lady of the Land, an admirable manager of the mansion, joined the anti-Peg forces. She was the wife of Major Andrew Jackson Donelson, the President's principal secretary, a nephew of Rachel, and together with Mary Eastin, Rachel's niece, she had kept things smooth at home, attending to her household duties, inviting the right people to the right affairs, receiving them, and returning their visits. Now suddenly both women said no. They acknowledged Andrew Jackson as head of the family, yes, and they would greet Mrs. Eaton when she came to the White House because she was then his guest, but they would not pay the required return visit.

The President directed Major Donelson to order his wife

to obey. Donelson refused. The President then had it out with Emily herself. Either she called upon Peggy Eaton or she went back to Tennessee.

Emily, a redhead, went back to Tennessee. Her husband went with her, and so did Mary Eastin.

Andrew Jackson was a fond family man, and he missed these daily reminders of Rachel, but his feelings had been hurt.

He faced many problems in those first tense days of his administration. There was the matter of national finances, for he firmly believed that the trend toward solvency should be continued and the debts left over from the War of 1812 paid off.

There was the question of the Cherokee people, whom Georgia had refused to recognize and treat with as a separate sovereign nation, as the federal government intended. What should be done about them and about all the other troublesome "civilized" tribes, who were prepared to resist any move to nudge them across the Mississippi?

There was the question of intrastate improvements—roads and canals chiefly—and whether the government should pay for them.

There was the small but frightening rumble of something being called "nullification" in the South, and especially in South Carolina, the richest state there and the land of the hotheads. Not "secession," heavens no, but "nullification" was bad enough.

There was the question of the Bank of the United States, which planned to ask for a renewal of its charter very soon.

There was the rift in his own party. Disagreements threatened to tear apart the whole fabric of government, with Henry Clay and his so-called American System, Daniel Webster as the darling of the money men, J. Q. Adams with the Federalist remnants still clinging to his coattails, and always the intellectual Mr. Calhoun, who never ceased to plot for the presidency.

But to none of these tremendous problems did Andrew Jackson give the time and thought that he gave to Peggy Eaton.

10

PANIC AT THE
PIE COUNTER

Had the Spoils System been called something else, anything else, it would not loom like a thundercloud over the record of Andrew Jackson. In fact, the Hero did call it something different. To him it was Rotation of Office. This name seems to suggest a picture of a contented, gossipy group of politicians, who from time to time, like the guests at the March Hare's tea party, all move over one place.

It didn't work out that way; the name Rotation of Office, a name that today would be hailed as a public relations triumph, did not stick, and the business instead has come down in history under the malodorous designation of Spoils System.

In pre-Revolution days when the thirteen American colonies first tried to work together and plan together in preparation for fighting together, the chief threat to this badly needed cooperation was the suspicion the men of Virginia, on one side, had of the men of Massachusetts, on the other. This suspicion, which was deep-seated and sore, was returned in kind. Delegates to the First and Second continental congresses from the Old Dominion found the nasal-voiced New Englanders uncouth, unco guid, "Levellers" who thought that they knew everything; "the Wise Men of the East," Virginians sneered.

These same Virginians were themselves sneered at by the

Yankees, who distrusted them and their precious primogeniture, their pride of position, their pretense of gentility. All Virginians, officially at least, were Episcopalians, and to the men of Massachusetts this was nearly as bad as being Catholic.

Snarling also occurred elsewhere in the colonies, and sometimes it almost broke into war. New Yorkers and Connecticut residents hated one another. New York and New Hampshire repeatedly were on the verge of violence over the ownership of the unfixed colony of Vermont. New York and Pennsylvania frequently squabbled over their western boundaries, and both of them exchanged harsh names with Virginia and North Carolina in the same matter.

But the Massachusetts-Virginia feud was the one that most immediately endangered the alliance, and it was to this that the farseeing forefathers of the United States turned their attention. Thus, when at an early session of the Second Continental Congress it became apparent that a new federal army should be created to take over from the various loose militia groups at the siege of Boston, it was John Adams, one of the wisest of the Wise Men of the East, one of the most vocal anyway, who sprang to his feet to place in nomination as commander in chief of this army the name of a Virginian, George Washington, a motion that was seconded by his cousin Samuel, the most fiery of the northern incendiaries and, in Virginian eyes, the most dangerous. It was the first great get-together act.

After the Revolution, after the adoption of the Constitution, the nation's first Secretary of State, Thomas Jefferson, perceived that Massachusetts had slipped from its position as the first power in the North, this position being taken by New York, the fastest-growing state. Jefferson perceived as well that a combination of New York and Virginia might ease the country away from Alexander Hamilton's crass commercial projects, with their glorification of the moneybags men, and toward his own unobtrusive but insistent claims for a narrower interpretation of the

Constitution, an agrarian state, and democracy. Moreover, this combination might do much to prevent a rift in the union, a split between North and South, which Jefferson even then fore-saw.

In the days when Philadelphia was the capital of the United States, and in the early years of Washington, D.C., the men of Albany and Richmond really ran things nationally. They were never as powerful as rumor painted them, but they did work well together, and until the coming of the Era of the Common Man, with Andrew Jackson and the death of the congressional caucus as a device for picking presidents, they did, undoubtedly, swing a lot of weight. The Old Dominion supplied the statesmen, as witness the shining lights of the Virginia Dynasty—Jefferson, Madison, Monroe—while New York supplied the practical politicians, such organizational masters as Aaron Burr, George Clinton, and, on the very eve of the Jacksonian Era, Martin Van Buren. It was in New York, city and state, that the political machine as we know it today was conceived, assembled, and first put to work, and it was there that it operated the smoothest. New York was the home of the Albany Regency, the members of which, according to popular belief, got their mysterious powers as a result of occult rites carried out in a clandestine manner in the depths of some enchanted grotto.

New York, too, had recently introduced a new insurance against loss of power: you threw out of office all those who couldn't be counted upon to vote for you again, replacing them with those who could. This practice might spread. From the moment when Andrew Jackson's election to the presidency was announced there were rumors in Washington that he would extend it, applying it on a national scale.

Fittingly, it was a New Yorker who gave this amazing new system (new, that is, to those who had never read Guicciardini or Machiavelli) a name.

William Learned Marcy, lately Governor of New York, made

his maiden speech in the United States Senate a spirited defense of the realistic methods used in his state.

> I know, sir, that it is the habit of some gentlemen to speak with censure or reproach of the politics of New York. Like other States, we have contests, and, as a necessary consequence, triumphs and defeats. The State is large, with great and diversified interests; and in some parts of it, commerce is the object of general pursuit; in others, manufacture and agriculture are the chief concerns of its citizens. We have men of enterprise and talents, who aspire to public distinction. It is natural to expect that from these circumstances and others that might be alluded to, that her politics should excite more interest at home, and attract more attention abroad, than those of many other States in the Confederacy.

So far, his only applause was yawns, and the galleries were empty, the Senate chamber itself almost so. But his peroration caused dissenting senators to sit up straight, for it gave the age a label, being an easily repeatable sniff of disparagement.

> It may be, sir, that the politicians of New York are not so fastidious as some gentlemen are as to disclosing the principles on which they act. They boldly preach what they practice. When they are contending for victory, they avow their intention of enjoying the fruits of it. If they are defeated, they expect to retire from office; and if they are successful, they claim, as a matter of right, the advantages of success. They see nothing wrong in the rule, that to the victor belongs the spoils of the enemy.

Many a time afterward Marcy could have bitten his tongue off for having let slip that sentence. But it was too late. The hated New York System had instantly become the Spoils System, and Andrew Jackson's rather pathetic "Rotation" was forgotten forever.

The problem the President faced here was by no means a new one. The Constitution had made no provision for political parties, something that the framers thought they could avoid.

The first twelve years of the new nation *as* a nation had been all Federalist, for the Federalists, who considered themselves the Chosen People and looked upon Thomas Jefferson and his strict construction disciples as out-and-out anarchists, had of course packed the various government departments with persons of their own persuasion, persons they could depend upon to vote their way—many of them, like the Supreme Court justices, in office for life.

Jefferson, when he became President in 1801, found himself surrounded by persons who disapproved of him and his methods and his friends. In those circumstances, he could hardly bring about the reforms he sought. Yet he had been elected on a pledge to do just that, to bring about those reforms. He was reluctant to oust any man from a government job for purely political reasons, yet obviously he could not continue with a team that was one hundred percent opposed to its captain. In those pre-Civil Service days the jobs in question were wholly his; he could do as he wanted with them. Of course he might fill vacancies with persons of his own party but "Few die and fewer still resign," he wailed. So he did some discharging. He was, of course, cursed for it.

Since that time the Federalists had been washed away in a flood of democratic feeling, and technically, on paper, only one party existed. Yet this party had been split, and still was splitting, so that Jackson, despite his thumping popular majority, was faced with ideological foes who were prepared to balk his every move, in Congress and out, who were prepared to play any dirty trick upon him that their consciences and the situation would permit, prepared too to scream "favoritism!" every time he seated a friend of his own in any governmental position. There were actually two parties in the United States, and sometimes three, occasionally four.

Since that early time, too, a couple of crashing differences clamored for attention:

First, the electorate had been enormously enlarged. Not only had many more states been taken into the Union, but those states and the old ones, with very few exceptions, had lowered their voting restrictions, while the population of the country as a whole was increasing all the time. In 1824, when Jackson first ran for President, fewer than one quarter of the adult white males could vote; in 1828, when he was elected, 56 percent of them could. The actual number of votes cast had almost quadrupled in those four years.

Second, the number of federal officeholders also had increased. One example: when Washington was inaugurated there were 75 post offices; when Jackson was inaugurated there were 7,600. All of these were within the President's power to do with as he wished.

He did what he thought he had to do. Perhaps he did not do it very well. He might have been too hasty. First complaints were concerned with the irregularity of the liquidation. The ax fell all right, but it fell in a seemingly haphazard manner, now here, now there, so that the fearful officeholder could not tell, when he went to work in the morning, whether or not he would return that night still an employee of the United States Government. It was not a clean sweep but rather a series of chops.

Consternation seized Washington, where the pen pushers flocked and twittered together like frightened pigeons on a roof. All sorts of stories swirled around—stories of how So-and-So after many years of faithful service, and after having just made the last payment on a house he had purchased in Washington, where he proposed to spend the rest of his life, suddenly found himself unemployed at the age of fifty-something, with nowhere to go and nothing to sell, and for no other reason, as far as he could make out, than that once, inadvertently, perhaps in the dark, he had passed a picture of President Jackson without pausing to make the proper bow. So-and-So had always considered that job his own, one from which he would never be jarred, and so did all the members of his family, and all his friends and well-wishers. The howl of rage was earsplitting.

"There has been a great noise made about removals," the arch-villain himself, Old Hickory, recorded in his private journal on May 18, 1829.

This is to be brought before Congress, with the propriety of passing a law vacating all offices periodically—then the good can be re-appointed, and the bad, defaulters, left without murmurs. Now, every man who has been in office a few years, believes he has a life estate in it, a vested right, and if it has been held twenty years or upwards, not only a vested right, but that it ought to descend to his children, and if no children then the next of kin. This is not the principles of our government. It is rotation in office that will perpetuate our liberty.

In other words, Jackson was trying to prevent the establishment of what a later generation would call the Establishment.

The slaughter was not great, though admittedly it was messy. The Rotation System, by whatever name it might be called, was not a holocaust. Only 600 postmasters and postmasters' deputies were ousted, out of almost 8,000. Of 612 other officials under the direct control of the President, only 252 were removed.

Moreover, though all removals were made without warning and without any sort of trial or hearing, all were not made without cause. The Hero's advance scouts had unearthed a great deal that was rotten in the public service, and it was chiefly at these places that the Hero slashed.

Thus, after Tobias Watkins, a friend of John Quincy Adams, had been removed from his post in the Treasury Department to make room for Jackson's seemingly sinister friend Amos ("The Goblin") Kendall, it turned out that Watkins had stolen $7,000 from the government, and he served a jail term for it.

The port collectors were especially loose in their methods; at Buffalo, Key West, Bath, Maine, and Portsmouth, New Hampshire, all turned out to be crooks after they were removed. The collector at Elizabeth City, North Carolina, skipped to Canada (with which we had no extradition treaty at the time) with

$32,791 in government money. So did the collector at Perth Amboy, New Jersey, but what *he* got away with was $80,000. Within eighteen months of the new administration its Rotation System had unveiled peculations of more than $280,000 in the Treasury Department alone.

Most of the new appointees were honest men. Nobody questioned it. However, there was one glaring exception. The choicest plum of all, the collectorship of the port of New York, went to a Jackson adherent, Samuel Swarthout, who a little later absconded to Europe with more than a million and a quarter.

The panic at the pie counter came to a climax—if not to an end—late in 1829, when John Henshaw, a Treasury Department clerk, who had just been given his pink slip, committed suicide. Somewhat later, when the friends of the President managed to make themselves heard above the moaning and groaning this caused, it was learned that Henshaw, who for years had suffered from chronic melancholia, twice before had attempted to kill himself. Nevertheless, Jackson was called a murderer.

"In recent years, the study of the spoils system has been marred by a tendency to substitute moral disapproval for an understanding of causes and necessities," writes Arthur M. Schlesinger, Jr. "There can be small doubt today that, whatever evils it brought into American life, its historical function was to narrow the gap between the people and the government—to expand popular participation in the workings of democracy. For Jackson it was an essential step in the gradual formulation of a program for democratic America."

When it was pointed out to the Hero, as so often it was, that he would lose a large handful of voters for every *fonctionnaire* he replaced, he shook an impatient head. Disappointed office seekers, he remarked, "are men who cry out principle, but who are on the scent of Treasury pap.

"If I had a tit for every one of these pigs to suck at," he went on, "they would still be my friends."

11

THEY CALLED HIM SHARP KNIFE

A down-at-moccasin-heels redskin, sober, but furtive and shifty-eyed, sidled up to a general, from whom he hoped to get employment as a scout. "Me good Indian," he mumbled.

"The only good Indians I ever saw were dead," the general replied.

This bit of wit, modified usually to "The only good Indian is a dead Indian," is attributed sometimes to William Tecumseh Sherman, who is better known for his march through Georgia, and sometimes to Edmund Pendleton Gaines, after whom both Gainesville, Florida, and Gainesville, Texas, are named, although sometimes too it is attributed to another Major General of the U.S. Army, Andrew Jackson.

None of these stories has any documentary backing, but the one about Jackson is demonstrably wrong. Jackson didn't hate Indians and didn't even despise them, as so many Tennesseans of his time did. He was not a racist, he was a realist.

In the early frontier days there had been many men who did indeed believe that the only good Indian was a dead one, and such persons customarily excused this belief with a story of how they had seen their mothers stripped and scalped before their eyes in some remote raid or had lain all night a prisoner in an Indian camp, forced to listen to the screams of other

111

prisoners whose skin was being torn out bit by bloody bit while their feet were slowly roasted.

Jackson probably understood the Indians as well as any man of his day. He was their kind of person. When he went against them he paid them the compliment of going with all his might, for he knew that in Indian eyes any touch of mercy, howsoever mild, was inexcusable. The redskin did not mind being killed—he expected as much if he was incapacitated in battle—but he would have wept in shame if he thought that the man who did it had been brushed, even briefly, by compassion. Jackson gave them what they wanted, and they respected him for it. They invited him to their councils. They listened when he spoke. They called him Sharp Knife, and they meant it as praise.

The goggle-eyed *wunderkinder* who cackle so smoothly at our cocktail parties these days have a new word of unspeakable contempt to replace the worn-out "communist." Anybody they don't like they call a racist. And the worst kind of racist—at least, the latest worst kind, perhaps because he is never at hand to defend himself—is the hater of Indians.

These reinterpreters of history would have us believe that all federal dealings with the Indians were fraught with fraud, that no treaty ever was made that was not immediately broken, and that the reason for all this villainy lay in the color of the victim's skin. Posing as sophisticates, they are the most gullible of the gullible. More fervently even than the immediate disciples of that expert on race relations, Jean Jacques Rousseau, they believe in the "noble savage" who can do no wrong. All, to them, is white on one side, black on the other. The complex story of race relations in the United States, as far as it pertains to the American Indian, is that of evil, avaricious men using guile, whiskey, false promises, and Iagoesque planted clues to bamboozle and degrade the innocent, unresting aborigine.

Andrew Jackson did not like the Indians as military allies,

as auxiliaries in the field, but that was not because he didn't trust them—he did—but because of their habit of celebrating a victory, even a petty one, by going back to their villages for a dance of triumph. This practice made an effective follow-up difficult if not impossible, for native scouts were a necessity in any wilderness campaign, and it spoiled a general's plans to have them gone.

Old Hickory did not, however, dislike them as *men*. On the contrary, he seemed to enjoy their company, and surely they enjoyed his, as they valued his advice, because time after time they invited him to attend powwows. The Indians of those times, although they had learned to be wary of land speculators, did not, as today's intellectuals maintain, believe that every white man talked with forked tongue, and certainly with Sharp Knife they always knew exactly where they stood. He believed that it would be best for them to cross the Mississippi and occupy the vast lands the government was offering them. He could have been wrong, but that is what he believed.

He said as much, clearly, in his first message to Congress. He favored the Georgian contention that, no matter what the previous commitments of the federal government, the Cherokees simply must be made to understand that independence within the bounds of a sovereign state was impossible, and that they, along with the Creeks, Choctaws, and Chickasaws, should be induced to cross the Mississippi (or "X the M," as Jackson put it in his letters) as soon as possible.

"But," the message added, "this emigration should be voluntary; for it would be as cruel as unjust to compel the aborigines to abandon the graves of their fathers, and seek a home in a distant land."

That word *voluntary* was interpreted loosely. The scandals connected with the great population shift were all on a local level and had to do largely with food supplies furnished the Indians on the way. This cheating, which often had fatal results, was the work of contractors, not of the usual federal Indian agents who for the most part were dedicated, honest men. Andrew Jackson had nothing to do with it, either.

The brand-new United States of America had almost got into a war with the Creeks early in George Washington's first administration. Georgia had wanted such a war—it would have been the nation's first—but didn't want to fight it, or pay for it, alone. Georgia applied to the new central government, then operating out of New York City. Washington more or less acceded to the demand, and assigned the first Secretary of War, fat, disagreeable young Henry Knox, to draw up a plan. This Knox did, and Washington approved the plan. The President, however, thought that one more effort—a direct effort, not one made through Georgia—should be made to placate the Creeks. Knox set about this by appointing a commission of distinguished men to call upon Alexander McGillivray, the "King of the Creeks."

This dark-eyed beanpole was not really a king at all, though he was certainly the most powerful of the Creek chiefs, and the richest as well, having at one time on his plantation on the Coosa, near the site of the present city of Montgomery, Alabama, at least sixty slaves, black escapees. He was not ferocious, as an Indian chief should be, but quiet in his ways, exceedingly fond of liquor, and so far from being a sanguinary fiend that he used to get sick at the mere sight of blood. But he was successful. To the Spaniards of New Orleans he was always the Creek spokesman, and he played the Spaniards' game well, as he spoke the Spaniards' tongue. He also played the fur game in collusion with the Scottish adventurers who represented English trading firms, usually based in the Bahamas. He spoke English too, but he didn't like Americans.

To the members of this latest commission Alexander McGillivray—though his tribal name was Hoboi-Hili-Miko, which means Good Child King—had explained yet again that he was not *the* chief of the Creeks but only *a* chief. He had inherited his considerable power from his mother, a celebrated half-breed beauty, Sehoy Marchand, whose father had been French. She was a Wind, and that made McGillivray a Wind too, for the Creek society was matriarchal.

The members of the commission nodded, unimpressed. They still wanted the chief to go to New York with them. He agreed at last, though he insisted upon taking no fewer than thirty fellow chiefs with him. Also, he refused to go by sea, the natural way. He had been at sea once, from Pensacola to New Orleans on a Spanish errand, and he had been sick. No more of that.

They made an eye-catching procession, with their wagons, their feathers and beads, their outriders. Richmond, Baltimore, Philadelphia gave them noisy greetings. There was only one water hop, the last leg—Elizabethtown, New Jersey, to the foot of Manhattan Island—and Hoboi-Hili-Miko endured this with a fitting stoicism.

They were met in style, and escorted by cavalry to the Executive Mansion, where President Washington greeted them with a speech they couldn't understand and gave each one a string of beads and a packet of tobacco. After that they repaired to the City Tavern for a feast, and each of them was made an honorary sachem of the newly formed Society of St. Tammany. That was July 20, 1790. The festivities lasted until August 14. From time to time, when a few responsible Indians could be rounded up—a few, that is, who were not momentarily doing a war dance in the street for drinks—there might be a business session, but for the most part Alexander McGillivray, who stayed admirably sober, did all the work. He was put up by Secretary of War Knox himself, in his house in Wall Street. Most of the others slept at the City Tavern or the Indian Head or Fraunces' place, and a few spread their blankets on the ground 'way up north near Canal Street.

115

The King of the Creeks was handed all sorts of medals and scrolls. He was elected an honorary member of the St. Andrew's Society. He was commissioned a brigadier general in the United States Army. He was appointed the federal Indian agent for the Lower Creek country, a job that paid $1,200 a year. And eventually he and General Knox hammered out an agreement by means of which the Indians would only lose a little of the land the Georgians craved, so that war was averted— or at least postponed. Then President Washington, though he hated to touch or be touched by any other man, personally shook hands with each of the thirty chiefs and thanked them, and they all went home.

Thus was started the tradition of the Great White Father. Every President from that time on, excepting Andrew Jackson, has followed Washington's example, and invited the Indians to come to him. Jackson went to them.

He had often been in their villages, sometimes for days together. When the Creek War at last did come, and Old Hickory lambasted the braves into submission, he dictated the terms of peace in a series of backwoods powwows, during which he, the victor, was almost unattended. He may have felt some fear on those occasions, but he never showed it, which is what counted with the Indians.

Now, as President of the United States, visiting his home in Tennessee, he heard that a large group of Cherokees was conferring with some of the principal Chickasaw chiefs at Dancing Rabbit Creek, not far from the Hermitage. He expected, and soon got, an invitation. He went. He had with him a Negro slave as coachman and a young half-breed friend who was to be an interpreter.

He greeted the braves gravely, and was so greeted. He smoked many a pipe with them, chatting with old friends, as he made the leisurely rounds. He delivered an oration.

After the first Creek War the victorious general when he

set forth his terms had had a fractured left shoulder, the result of the Benton brothers fracas in Nashville, and had carried his arm in a sling. At the Chickasaw-Cherokee conference, the sling no longer was there, though Jesse Benton's bullet still was, and General Jackson, then as before, was suffering from rheumatism, either chronic constipation or dysentery, and recurrent malaria. The greatest pain of all, though, must have been in the delivery of that speech to the Indians. He hated even ordinary, everyday public speaking, and the Indians, as he well knew, would expect him to go on, with the utmost solemnity, for hours. This he did. It was his duty.

That few of them could understand a word he said, and few could even hear him, didn't matter. The half-breed boy shouted each sentence in several different Muskogean dialects, giving the Great White Father a chance to frame the next ponderous inanity before he launched it at a delighted if deadpan audience.

Afterward he greeted again sundry old war companions, Opothleyoholo, Tustenneggee, Mushulatubbe—he remembered their names. Then he got back into his carriage and was driven off.

The Chickasaws agreed to "X the M," and the Cherokees agreed at least to think it over.

Undoubtedly President Jackson sympathized with the State of Georgia in its efforts to get rid of its Indians. He thought it would be best for all concerned if every redskin in the Southwest Territory were moved across the Father of Waters. Yet when it came to a showdown between Georgia's claims and the views of the United States Supreme Court, he wavered. The matter was brought to a head by the arrest of two New England missionaries, Samuel A. Worcester and Elizur Butler. These two had been living among the Cherokees, on Cherokee land, and when the Georgia legislature passed a law requiring all such residents to take an oath of allegiance to the state—and the state

117

alone—they refused. They were imprisoned. The church lawyers got busy, and soon the Supreme Court in Washington issued a writ of error, which a federal marshal served on the governor. The governor, denying the Supreme Court's authority here, refused to act upon it, and the legislature instructed local peace officers to decline to obey the order from Washington.

On February 1832 the case was heard in Washington before the Supreme Court—and a full audience. The State of Georgia was not represented, though it had of course been notified. The Supreme Court, headed by that stubborn Federalist holdover, Chief Justice John Marshall, reversed the judgment of the Georgia court and issued a mandate calling for the release of Worcester and Butler.

"John Marshall has made his decision—now let him enforce it," Andrew Jackson is supposed to have cried when he read the court order. It could be true. The statement, however, rests upon an editorial written many years afterward by a brilliant but no means reliable young newspaper editor named Horace Greeley, who was working for the new Whig party, an organization that owed its existence to anti-Jacksonism. It could be true, though. No doubt Jackson felt that way.

The federal government never did try to enforce that Supreme Court order. The missionaries Butler and Worcester served several months in the Georgia state penitentiary, an uncomfortable place, and then were sent back to New England. Congress by close votes in both houses appropriated $500,000 and authorized the President to negotiate removal treaties with all tribes still east of the Mississippi. Georgia, clearly, had won. Atlanta had defied Washington, and prevailed.

But race hatred in the White House? That is a recent theory, originated and promulgated by the *wunderkinder* of the cocktail parties, who seemingly never heard of Lincoyer.

Lincoyer had been a barely discernable spot of flesh amid the ruins of burned huts, amid the dead bodies of Indians, after the fight at Horseshoe Bend. He was very small and his cry was very faint, yet the General heard and heeded it. The General's dysentery was acting up, and he was so sick that he couldn't ride a horse and was being carried around the battlefield by two aides, while he gave orders for the final slaughter and the chase. He sent one of the aides to seek out the baby, and he took it back to Tennessee, to the Hermitage, where he and Rachel formally adopted it, their fourth adopted child, the other three being white. It might be mentioned that this happened before the battle of New Orleans, long before Jackson could be thought to harbor presidential aspirations. The adoption of the baby was no political act. He and Rachel christened it Lincoyer, after one of her relatives.

Lincoyer was pure Creek, no half-breed. He went to school with the other three boys and ate with them and their parents. When he died of tuberculosis at the age of sixteen, he was buried in the family plot. Surely not racism.

12

CHESTNUT STREET
OR WALL?

What does a great fighting man do when there's nobody to fight, when all his opponents have been knocked flat, though he himself, scarcely panting, hasn't even got up a good sweat?

Old Hickory looked around. From 1600 Pennsylvania Avenue, Washington, D.C., it was hard to see anything that still needed walloping, for he seemed already to have won whatever he wanted. But he persisted, and when he remembered the Bank of the United States he gave a whoop of battle joy and waded in, both arms swinging. Now he was happy again.

He had picked a formidable opponent. Many men have wondered, since then, why. Books have been written on the subject.

Andrew Jackson had done his share of land gambling, and had suffered his share of bad luck. Had he been a man for self-pity he might have moaned that he had been "stung" by the system, for in fact his investments did seem unlucky, most of them. Close friends of about his own age, his own station in life, in similar surroundings and with similar opportunities—men like John Coffee, John Overton, John Donelson III—made substantial fortunes, while the Hero barely survived. But he did not blame the Bank of the United States for this.

It must be believed, then, that at least in the beginning

Old Hickory's opposition to the Bank of the United States was based upon his belief as a good Jeffersonian that it was unconstitutional. It was, in his eyes, wrong. The government should not have to hire a private company to handle its financial affairs for it.

The Bank had been started, in the early days of the republic, by the first Secretary of the Treasury, Alexander Hamilton. It was one of the four conditions Hamilton insisted upon to put the federal government on what he considered a good sound business basis—that is, in debt. A public debt, Hamilton asserted, could be a public blessing.

The Bank was authorized to handle all the federal government's fiscal matters, including the minting of money. One fifth of its stock would be held by that government, the other four fifths by private interests. It was chartered to operate for sixteen years.

This was, of course, in accord with Hamilton's belief that the rich should run the country. Rich men should be lured into government somehow, by acquisition of federal bonds that carried a high interest guarantee, by a promise of high tariff rates on any product they were interested in, by being given—or practically given—a controlling interest in the banking machinery. His whole system was based upon this assumption. As John Jay, one of his most ardent supporters, put it, "The men who own the country ought to govern it."

So, with only a slight bending of Mr. Hamilton's doctrine of implied powers, the Bank of the United States came into being. The Jeffersonians, who were strict constructionists—that is, they believed that the Constitution meant exactly what it said, neither more nor less—were horrified. However, there was nothing that they could do, even after they had come into power with the election of 1800, unless the BUS grossly violated the conditions of its charter, and the BUS didn't.

Then came the War of 1812, which was unfortunate for

121

all concerned, except, to be sure, Andrew Jackson. The federal government, which under Jefferson and in the early Madison years had heroically pulled itself out of debt, was plunged once more into a financial morass. Indeed, in 1815, when the shooting was over, the United States teetered on the verge of bankruptcy. Something must be done to avert ruin, something drastic. So the Bank was revived. It was chartered again, in 1816, for twenty years, to the tune of $35,000,000, one fifth of which was to be owned by the government, four fifths by the public. Of the $20,800,000 in private hands, more than one quarter was owned by foreigners, 383 of them. Over $16,000,000, or more than half of the total stock now owned by the government, was in the hands of 822 men, while the remaining U.S. private stockholders, largely widows, orphans, and the trustees of charity funds, held only a little over $3,000,000 worth.

In other words, big money men would control the Bank, which was as Alexander Hamilton, long since in his grave, had wanted it.

The Bank was a corporation, the biggest corporation in the United States, one of the biggest in the world.

The price of its stock on the open market varied from 120 to 125¾, but when Andrew Jackson, the new President, sent his first message to Congress—a message that, unexpectedly, contained a virtual declaration of war against the Bank—it went down to 116. Soon, however, it climbed back, which could only be because the moneybag men had decided, after thinking it over, that President Jackson didn't mean that threat at all.

The first Bank of the United States, after which the Second Bank of the United States was modeled, allowed for great power at the top. Its head was the only one of the twenty-five directors who was allowed to serve for more than three years running. He appointed all the committees. He dictated policy. He was, in effect, the Bank.

The first president of the rechartered institution, a Southerner, William Jones, who served in 1818 and part of 1819, almost put it into its grave before a proper start could be made. He was too good-natured. He was succeeded by Langdon Cheves, also a Southerner, but a Southerner who might have been born to be a banker, he was so superbly equipped to say no. Cheves very soon had the Second Bank of the United States on its feet and going full speed ahead. He lasted until 1822.

And then came Nicholas Biddle.

"Figures don't lie," our grandfathers were fond of telling us, and to this it might be countered that liars figure. Nicholas Biddle had barely turned thirty-nine when he was elected to the country's highest banking post, and that in itself was held against him by the high priests of the inner circle, who unabashedly avowed that no banker—no proper banker—should ever be so young. He was a member of the club, and in public they of course supported him, but they shook their heads as they did so. Even today's most respected historian of the American banking system, Bray Hammond, looks upon Biddle as an amateur, who "was too fond of playing a role and acting like a banker instead of being one." He goes on.

> Mr. Biddle had what experience alone could never give, but he lacked what it could give. There had been nothing in his singularly happy, protected, and productive career to develop defenses against the nonintelligent or provide him with the earthy faculty of give and take. He had had no practical administrative experience of any sort, he had never known reverses or disfavor or the discipline of an organization, he had struggled for nothing that he possessed. He had not had to put up with superiors who were his inferiors. He had not learned to share responsibilities with others. He liked being irresistible. He had been admired by friends and untroubled by enemies. He was governed by consideration and reason and had the untempered intellectual's preference for what ought to be over what is.

Personally everybody loved the man, everybody lucky enough

123

to know him. He was a prodigy without any of the prodigy's aloofness. His attraction was without strain. He had graduated from Princeton at the age of fifteen, head of his class. He liked to write light verse. He had dabbled in literature and in diplomacy. He had inherited some money, married more, worked for none. He had built himself a lovely estate on the Delaware, knew everybody worth knowing, had even started to write a novel. Although he had been elected to the presidency of the Bank as something of a reformer—he was the head of a party of Young Turks determined to turn out the far-right Cheves—his was essentially a conservative position. He was a Biddle, after all. His closest friend was a Cadwallader—Thomas, of Philadelphia.

He was a linguist, a dandy, a mathematician. Certainly he was destined for some high post, some important mission, though for many years his associates and the members of his family could not guess what this might be. He had edited the Lewis and Clark journals, a stupendous task. He had made a digest of the laws of foreign nations affecting United States commerce, his sources being English, French, Spanish, German, Italian, and Dutch, for he spoke all of these languages. He also played the piano.

The original BUS had worked well. Nobody questioned that. The only apparent reason why its charter had not been renewed in 1811 was the prevailing belief among Jeffersonians, who were in power, that it was unconstitutional. Since that time two full-length moves to kill the Bank through state action designed to tax all branch banks out of existence had been stepped upon by the Supreme Court. *McCulloch* v. *Maryland,* 1819, and *Osborn* v. *United States Bank,* 1824, had seemed to establish the legitimacy of the business. Both of these decisions, however, had been written by Chief Justice Marshall, and Jeffersonians still hoped that if ever this hard-shell tory expired—for he sometimes seemed immortal—they could perhaps get them reversed.

CHESTNUT STREET OR WALL?

The second BUS, once the Jones presidency had been terminated, was even more sensationally successful. It raised money readily. It opened branches. It built a new building in Philadelphia, on the south side of Chestnut Street between Fourth and Fifth streets, a showplace, one of the nation's first Greek Revival structures, which drew more attention than the old State House, recently renamed Independence Hall, one square to the west of it.

Londoners were fond of calling their Bank of England headquarters the Old Lady of Threadneedle Street. Americans were harsher with the Bank of the United States main office: they called it the Monster of Chestnut Street.

Parenthetically, many who called it that were New Yorkers. In the dog-eat-dog world of American banking everything was supposed to be expressible in figures; everything was mathematical. In fact, at this time personalities had a great deal to do with the management of banking, as did regional circumstances. New York City a little while ago had climbed past the 300,000 population mark, passing Philadelphia to become the biggest city in the nation. (After them came, in order, Baltimore, Boston, Charleston, New Orleans, Cincinnati or "Porkopolis," and Albany.) Wall Street, once a quiet residential thoroughfare, was shaping up as the financial capital of the country, challenging Chestnut Street. There was a great deal of feeling between these two places.

Nicholas Biddle—it was perhaps an example of what the old-timers, the orthodox bankers, called his "egregrious naïveté"—declared that the Bank of the United States had not meddled in politics. Even he, however, was obliged to admit that politics sometimes had meddled with the Bank. Members of Congress and other personages who might have power appeared never to meet difficulty in raising a loan at the Bank, or in repeatedly renewing one, howsoever slight the collateral they might put up. On the other hand, Westerners—so they

125

claimed, anyway—were deprived of what would have been their normal credit. The men of the West, who were almost unanimously behind Andrew Jackson in this as in so many other things, contended that the Eastern bankers—that is, the BUS— were driving independent Western bankers to the wall. The BUS people contended that they alone stood against a rising tide of paper money that the Western banks were issuing helter-skelter. Destroying the Bank of the United States in order to expel paper money, they declared, would be like killing the cat to keep the mice away.

Mississippi's seventeen state banks had circulated more than $6,000,000 in notes, although they had a total of only $303,000 in their various vaults. Andrew Jackson must have known this, and he was a hard-money man, opposed to paper money of less than $5 value. He had not proposed any substitute for or successor to the Second Bank of the United States. It was one of the weaknesses of his case.

Biddle's associates advised him to ignore the threat against the Bank implied in the President's first message to Congress. It was mere vaporing, they said. The President was obliged to talk tough for the benefit of the Western land speculators who had elected him. He would forget it soon and so would they. The Bank could then apply for renewal of its charter.

Biddle was not so sure. He had never met a man he couldn't charm into a state of babbling acquiescence. So he went to Washington, an onerous trip, and asked for an audience with the President. It was granted.

These two men fascinated one another. Though he must have been warned against such a preconception, Nicholas Biddle surely went to the White House tense with expectancy, thinking that he was about to tussle with some hairy savage, a belching, tobacco-chewing misanthrope who never had known, even from a distance, the finer things in life. That he was wrong came as a shock, but a pleasant one.

Andrew Jackson had no use for compromise; he was an

all-or-nothing man, who preferred all. Yet so exquisite were his manners and so seemingly sincere his sympathy on this occasion, that although the President promised nothing, the Tyrant of Chestnut Street—Czar Nicholas, his enemies in the press liked to call him—left the Executive Mansion aglow with confidence. Everything, he was sure, would be all right. There was a gentleman, if ever he had met one, and Nicholas Biddle knew how to handle gentlemen. The Second Bank of the United States, he was convinced, would get its renewal whenever it cared to apply for same.

He was mistaken. Andrew Jackson, despite the pleasure he had gained in the visit of this young man, had not the slightest thought of giving up his fight against the bank.

He was in a better position now to devote all of his energies to it. Things at the mansion were smooth again. Matty Van was no longer there to stage-manage social affairs, being in London as U.S. Ambassador to the Court of St. James's, but Emily, blessed Emily, was back, and so was her husband, the President's personal secretary, Andrew Jackson Donelson.

The war over Peggy Eaton is sometimes called the only war that Old Hickory ever lost. This is not fair. A draw would be a more accurate appraisal.

When it became apparent that nobody would budge and that very soon the news of the cabinet split must become public, the President had acted at last. He accepted the resignation of the Secretary of State (indeed, Van Buren was to assert in his memoirs that *he* had suggested the whole dodge, offering it to the President on one of those rides out on the Tenallytown Road, but this should be taken with a grain of salt) and then those of Ingham and Branch, while Berrien, who had been out of town, submitted his resignation on June 19, 1831, these following naturally and without embarrassment to either party involved. Eaton himself had already bowed out, and of the original cabinet only Barry, its weakest member, remained.

The new cabinet was stronger than the first one, if not

more "respectable," and inspired more confidence in the public. It consisted of Edward Livingston, the nation's leading constitutional authority, one of its best writers as well, as Secretary of State; Lewis Cass, for a long time governor of the vast Northwest Territory, Secretary of War; Lewis McLane, back from St. James's, Secretary of the Treasury; Levi Woodbury of New Hampshire, Navy; Roger Taney, Attorney General; and Barry.

The tenseness over the succession could be eased.

At the last minute, and after all resignations had been accepted and most office cleaning-out had been done, Eaton and the Quaker Ingham almost spoiled everything by getting into a scrape about Peg herself, Eaton contending that Ingham had libeled his wife and Ingham denying it, Eaton trying to jockey the other into a duel and Ingham ducking out in a most ignominious manner, leaving Washington forever in a curtained carriage long before dawn one day. This matter did get out, but in a version that only caused the public to laugh.

Thus, the United States survived its first cabinet turnover. The ship of state sailed on.

It had been necessary to get Van Buren far away, in order to persuade the Calhounites—Berrien, Ingham, and Branch—to step out. The British embassy had been a natural choice. Every snob wanted that job. Marty Van's friends urged him to refuse it, arguing that to be so far from Washington could mean the end of his political career, but he tuttutted this, sailing away gaily with an amusing young literary light from New York, Washington Irving, as his secretary. (The Jackson administration was kind to more than one aspiring writer who sought time in which to develop his talents: Nathaniel Hawthorne, William Cullen Bryant, and Herman Melville were similarly favored.)

Eaton was another matter, and presented a problem. At last a place that he and Peggy were willing to accept was found: the Spanish embassy. The court in Madrid was rigidly religious, and the teehee-ers in Washington predicted that Peg would soon disgrace us. But she was a tremendous hit.

Years later, after the Eatons had returned, they lived quietly in Washington, where he died in 1856, leaving Peggy a rich woman. She did not remain rich long. At Marini's dancing school in Washington, where Peg took her daughter for lessons, there was a dashing young instructor, one Antonio Buchighani, and he fell in love with them—both of them, or so he said—and in 1859 he was married to Bellona, the ex-toast of the town, the Aspasia of Washington, D.C. He got her money, or most of it, and then ran off with her daughter.

13

SHOTS AT A KING

When you shoot at a king, goes an old saying, you must not miss. His enemies at first did not refer to the seventh President of the United States as a king or any other manner of monarch, for the man's immense popularity could not be denied and any such designation might be taken as slander. Instead they peppered his less flavorsome friends, and here they were on firm ground, for the fear of a possible royal favorite still was loud in the land. Matty Van and the Kitchen Cabinet cronies were called the names. The Hero himself was deemed untouchable.

This soon changed. If Andrew Jackson disappointed the ill-wishers by failing to growl and grind his teeth at the slightest provocation, behaving instead in a quiet, sedate manner, he very soon did give them some excuse to clamor that he was seeking to usurp authority rightfully not his, as one might expect of a hot-tempered military man. Not in public, not aloud, but in the privacy of their congressional messes, in their boardinghouse parlors, the politicians began to refer to him as His Majesty, or King Andrew, sometimes as Andrew the First. Cartoonists took it up, and were open about it. They drew the President as a lanky figure asprawl on a throne, crown on his head, scepter in his hand. The picture, like the nickname, never really took on, but opposition politicians kept trying.

In fact, the Hero was exceedingly careful about his relations with the two houses of Congress, watchful of any possible infringement upon their prerogatives. The executive and the legislative were two separate departments, and he meant to keep them so. Like George Washington, as general and as President, he leaned over backward to assure congressmen that he was minding his own business.

Despite the insistence of all concerned that there was only one political party in the United States, the opposition to the Jackson group constantly strove to coagulate. It tried to be all things to all men, and was rent with internal dissensions. Part of the problem was that it had no central, positive reason for existence, only a dislike of and distrust of the Hero of New Orleans and all that he stood for, whatever that was. The mixup, the confusion, were brought about also because there were almost as many leaders as followers, and they led, or tried to lead, in almost as many directions. The government of the United States had degenerated into an unmannerly scramble for the top job. Nothing else mattered. You were not for or against a policy, a method, a creed; you were for or against a man.

The President never did try to bully Congress, as many had predicted he would do. He never scoffed at its weeks-long, turgid "debates," no matter how silly they might be, and he never scolded Congress for being slow, obstructive. But he watched it. At every session there was somebody either in the balcony or on the floor who was busy taking notes for a report to the master of 1600 Pennsylvania Avenue later that same afternoon or night.

Night sessions were frequent then. Major Lewis, who lived at the White House, customarily covered them, and no matter how late he was getting home, the President would be waiting for him and would listen to all the details. The President never slept well anyway. He drank very little, but he smoked whenever possible, and he was always gulping coffee. The doctors ordered him to give up coffee and tobacco, but he refused. He would rather suffer, he said.

The trouble with the opposition groups was that they could

not agree on anything except their dislike of Andrew Jackson. They did not really constitute a party. They were no more than that many splinters, a disarranged cluster. But when it came to hatred of the Hero of New Orleans, they were the very models of cooperation. They *needed* watching.

For most, indeed, for virtually all of the time Jackson was in office, the administration had a slight but firm majority in the House of Representatives, the opposition a slight but firm majority in the Senate. Only four of the states—Vermont, Massachusetts, Connecticut, and Delaware—had anti-Jackson legislatures. The legislatures did not greatly matter to the politicos of Washington. In those days it was still the custom for the federal government to permit the individual states to exercise unhampered the rights and privileges guaranteed them, as many thought, by the Constitution. The houses of Congress were another matter.

The House of Representatives had been the more important house of Congress at first, at least in their own eyes. The fact that revenue bills must originate in their chamber seemed to give the representatives superior status. It was in the House that great national figures first put forth their views about the government. Nobody was amazed when John Quincy Adams, after being refused a second term as President, got himself elected to the House of Representatives, where he served—"Old Man Eloquence"—for many years.

This situation, however, was changing. The senators, who had always thought of *their* chamber as the important one, had at first been a small, exclusive group, and quiet. They had acted in secret, eschewing publicity. The thought that any of the populace might be permitted to hear part of their discussions, much less to judge them for their usefulness, would have been repugnant to the early senators. By the time King Andrew ascended to the throne, however, the Senate had opened its portals to one and all, its members thrilled to have their words go forth

to an admiring world. They even had a spectators' gallery of
their own, one that was often crowded.

The senators' conviction of their special importance was
born of the memory of the provincial council, a feature in
virtually every one of the colonies. This council was usually
the royal governor's advisory body, not a noisy forum but rather
a select group of wealthy personages. The property requirements
for membership were much higher than those of the popular
legislative body, whatever that was called. The council met in
secret; it never published its discussions or even its vote; it was
answerable only to the governor himself, who in those days,
basking in light from above as the personal representative of
the British King, was just about infallible.

Surfaced, public property now, the new senators, once they
had got used to the glare, gloried in the yammer of politics,
and they, more than any other group, refined and at the same
time expanded that characteristic political tactic of the time—the
long speech.

The long speech was by no means confined to the halls
of the legislature, state or federal. It was heard everywhere. It
was the people's principal form of entertainment, of edification
as well, easily outdistancing the journal, the newsletter, and the
magazine, perusal of which was confined, after all, to intellectuals. People had more time in those days, when their political
rallies were held out of doors. Especially in the West and in
the South they thought nothing of traveling all morning, from
dawn to dinnertime, to a meeting place, where they would listen
all afternoon to one or at the most two speakers. They invariably
did this *standing.* It was not the custom to provide chairs at
political rallies.

Three hours was par for the course, although many could
do better than that. A man who could shout for three hours,
while shaking his fists or windmilling his arms, was a man to
be respected and even cheered. What he said didn't matter. How

long he took to say it did. A four-hour speech, obviously, was just that much more wonderful than a three-hour speech.

The United States Senate, with the most time of all, having only the affairs of the nation to attend to, naturally enjoyed this new oratorical form. Days rather than mere hours became the unit of speech measurement in the Senate. Goethe used to say that whenever he had a sorrow he made a poem, which caused Gameliel Bradford to remark that whenever Henry Clay had a sorrow he made a speech. The speeches of Senator Clay—for Clay was in the Senate now, after for so many years ruling the representatives' roost—were duly celebrated. Most of them were meant to seem extemporaneous, though in truth they had been carefully prepared and rehearsed.

The galleries, when Clay spoke, invariably were crowded, nor did any lady leave until he had finished, be it four or five or even six hours later. What did he speak about? It didn't matter. His colleague, Shepperd of North Carolina, "rather snappishly" remarked that Clay "could get more men to run after him to hear him speak, and fewer to vote for him, than any man in America."

The greatest favorite of the gallery gods, the marathon orator *par excellence,* was not a Westerner, nor yet a Southerner, but a man from New England, Daniel Webster. Of all the minnows who threshed about in the congressional tank in the belief that they were whales, he was the most impressive. It could be said of him, as Lemuel Gulliver said of the emperor of Lilliput, "He is taller by almost the breadth of my nail than any of his court, which alone is enough to strike an awe into the beholders."

Because of the complexion of his face rather than that of his heart, Webster had been called Black Dan at Dartmouth. The irreverent on Capitol Hill referred to him as the Archangel, a designation he might have thought belittling. His wrath was volcanic. Like Borria Bungalee Boo, that man-eating African swell, "His sigh was a hullaballoo, His whisper a horrible yell—A horrible, horrible yell!" Even when sober, he affixed his face into a vengeance-is-mine-saith-the-Lord scowl. When for the first time he turned those great, luminous, reproachful eyes upon a given man, that man distinctly if fleetingly felt that he had died and was about to be judged. Webster did have a large vocabulary, and of course a classical education. Also, unexpectedly, he had a sense of humor, but he seldom let it show.

When one of these senatorial geysers of pishposh felt an eruption coming on he would ask for and be granted permission to make a few remarks, no matter what business happened to be before the chamber at just that time, and it was impossible to silence him, or even slow him, once he had started to talk. Thus, early in the Jackson administration, on a dour January day of 1830, after Senator Foote of Connecticut had offered a resolution having something to do with the disposal of federal lands in the West, Robert Young Hayne, a South Carolina lawyer, rose to ask for, and be granted, the floor.

He spoke all that day, the nineteenth. He said very little about the Foote resolution, but being a follower of Calhoun, he held forth on the emerging Southern conception of the United States Constitution as, in fact, a compact between the states, a sort of gentlemen's agreement, rather than a sacred obligation.

All this while the senator from Massachusetts was seen to twist in his seat, to shake his head, and to cluck his tongue, frowning that famous frown. It was clear that he disagreed with the senator from South Carolina and longed to say so—out loud. The next morning, then, and without even having asked for it, he was given the floor. And *he* talked all of *that* day.

He said that everything that Senator Hayne had said was wrong. He explained why.

His speech drew the biggest crowd the Senate had ever known. Not only were the galleries filled with feminity—that was to be expected when one of the mighty ones was scheduled to speechify—but men who were friends of senators were standing in the back of the chamber and even, some of them, in the aisles.

On the twenty-first, Senator Hayne returned to the attack, and he was in fine form. Once again the place was packed. The senator talked all day.

A weekend intervened, while all Washington buzzed, nothing else being discussed in the barrooms, the parlors, the boardinghouse messes. Nobody even *thought* of anything else.

Hayne held the floor on the twenty-fifth, and he kept it all day. The following day it was Webster's turn again; he used every minute of it.

Both men had gone about as far as a speaker could go along the lines of magniloquence. They had fairly rolled in rodomontade, they had reveled in rant. Yet both came up to the scratch on the twenty-seventh full of words, *bursting* with words. They split this day between them. Black Dan got the last shout. Head back, his right arm sawing the air before him, the left arm, with closed fist, clenched into the small of his back, he roared, "Liberty and Union, now and forever, one and inseparable!"

After that they quit, not because they were exhausted but because the audience was.

The Foote resolution? It had become lost somewhere in the scuffle. It never was voted upon.

Historians have sometimes called this the United States Senate's finest hour, forgetting, it would seem, that it took almost an entire week.

It is a military convention that each arm of the service must meet and defeat the enemy's similar arm before a real battle can be joined. That is, the cavalry must drive the opposing cavalry from the field, or, today, the planes must drive all opposing planes from the air, before the infantry is sent forth to clash with its real and only enemy, the infantry forces of the other side.

The long-speech men were, in effect, the opposition's heavy artillery, so General Jackson, a stickler for military tradition, naturally brought up equally long-winded orators to offset them. Heavy artillery against heavy artillery; the rest could be figured out later. As he had done in the case of the Creeks, Andrew Jackson showed that he was not afraid—indeed, he welcomed the chance—to fight the foe with that foe's own methods.

His adjutant in the Senate, his field commander there, was none other than Thomas Hart Benton, whom once, long ago, General Jackson had caused to fall backward down the cellar steps of a Nashville hotel.

The Bentons, uncle and nephew, Thomas Hart and Jesse, the young man who had brought about the fracas by getting himself shot in the seat of the pants, had decided that Tennessee was no longer a healthy place for them, and when they got out of the hospital they moved to Missouri, where they did very well for themselves, Colonel Benton becoming, among other things, a United States senator. He was also retained as full-time lawyer for the rich American Fur Company, which always had favors to seek in Washington. He was the father of four daughters, the youngest of whom, Jessie, married John Charles Fremont, the Pathfinder, who was to become the Republican party's first nominee for President of the United States. (The senator was also to become the great-uncle of the artist who bore that same name, Thomas Hart Benton.)

It might have been hard, just at first, to take Thomas Hart Benton seriously. He looked a clown, and not infrequently acted that way. He might have been the original model for the cartoonists' United States senator—bellow, paunch, frock coat, politician's haircut, scowl, everything but the shoestring tie, a refinement that had not yet been introduced into the Capitol. He was not tall—he was of medium height—but he was big. He thundered. He had broad shoulders, knobby fists, long arms, and a deep chest. He had a lion's mane, a leonine head.

Harriet Martineau, she of the huge ear trumpet, found him "fantastic."

Though he could talk as long and as loudly as the best of them, and showed great skill in the arrangement of his forensic points, he was not eloquent. The galleries of the Senate chamber customarily were emptied when he rose to speak. He was not fussy about his facts, and would clout the enemy with any club he could lay hands on. Like his friend and one-time feuding foe, Andrew Jackson, he never had been to college; yet he could hurl classical allusions with the best of them, and not just the old standbys—Ariadne's thread, an eye for Polyphemus, *Carthago delenda est*, etc.—but every now and then a new and startling one, such as the time he referred to Clay's proposed Latin-American alliance as "a sort of confederacy or Amphictyonic council," which would send the learned ones scurrying to their libraries in the hope (always vain) of proving him wrong.

On the floor Benton was lumpy, but if he was not felicitous of speech at least he was alert, he was wary; he was the administration's watchdog in the Senate, always there, always prepared to growl, even to bite. He could be verbose when verbosity was called for, and he could speak all morning and all afternoon any time, for he seemingly never had to go to the bathroom. He was a master of parliamentary procedure. He never nodded. By his own count, at one session of Congress—and it was a short session—he spoke thirty times on one issue alone. That issue was, of course, the Bank. About the Bank, as about so many other things, he felt exactly as his chief did.

Thomas Hart Benton, in other words, was a good man to have on your side.

14

SOMETHING TO SHAKE A STICK AT

In the matter of men's fashions this was the period of the nobby beaver hat, tight trousers, short jackets with very thin tails, snuffboxes (with Maccoby in them, if you were an *aficionado*), and extra-long walking sticks.

The walking stick, shoulder-high some of them, must be taken seriously, for it was more than a fad, more than just a means of introducing a certain kind of fashionable languor into one's walk; it was a symbol of gentility; it marked the man who carried it as one who must be treated with respect.

For many years the sword had served this purpose. The short sword, the so-called court sword, degenerate successor of the Spanish rapier, had throughout the eighteenth century and even briefly into the nineteenth been an integral part of a gentleman's wardrobe. No one who respected his position would think of going out in public without a sword strapped to his side any more than he would have thought of going out without a coat on his back or a bunch of lace at his chin. The sword bespoke authority. It represented a readiness to resent any slight, however slight, and the means—the muscle perhaps, or the family connections, or the money—to make that resentment felt.

The sword indeed outlasted the wig as an article of male decoration.

The days of d'Artagnan were long gone. Fencing academies still existed, but very few of them. The average man who strapped on a sword before attending some formal ceremony, even the average military man, probably didn't know how to hold the thing properly, even assuming that he could pull it out of its scabbard without cutting himself. He carried it for purposes of identification, not protection. "Lug it out, sirrah!" was a cry no longer heard in the land. Yet a portrait painter would not even start to "do" a subject unless and until the sword was in place, and as late as 1796, when "His Rotundancy," the highly unmartial John Adams, was inaugurated as the second President of the United States, although he did not even wear a wig he carried a sword as a matter of course, looking the more ridiculous with it because he was obliged to stand beside the outgoing President, tall, erect George Washington, who might have been born with a sword at his side.

The walking stick, the cane, at the time of its first incarnation in the United States, was more of a weapon than the court sword had been. To be sure, the two were combined for a little while, but only here and there, briefly. The sword-cane, like the quizzing glass, never really took on in America, where it was regarded at best as an amusing novelty.

There used to be much talk of "horsewhipping" editors, political opponents, and other undesirable persons, and sometimes it was even done. Indeed, the verb "to bulldoze," before the invention of the earth-moving machine, is supposed to have come from "giving a bull's dose to"—that is, "giving a dose of the bullwhip to"—but no gentleman ever considered the whip a proper weapon, as it certainly wasn't a *convenient* weapon, with which to chastise an underling. The cane was more appropriate.

Andrew Jackson never went abroad in the daytime without a walking stick, and the custom came into being to watch for him to raise it, especially when he had just encountered a new or an ancient foe, of which he had many. In Washington they still talked of the time, just after the House of Representatives had pronounced John Quincy Adams President, when these two came face to face. The incident occurred at an evening affair, so that Old Hickory carried no cane, of course, but even so, he disappointed the audience by the quietness of his hello.

At least as exciting, though as much of a letdown, was the time he met Winfield Scott, commander in chief of the U.S. Army. They had differed, at long distance, about some minor matter of precedence, and the fiery Tennessean had sent to his superior a letter that in effect was a challenge. General Scott with great good sense had replied that the matter was not worth quarreling about and that he and his correspondent, after what they had done at Lundy's Lane and at New Orleans, did not need to redemonstrate their courage. At the time Jackson, much talked of for the presidency, was in Washington as a fill-in senator, as was Scott as head of the army, and a man who was never unaware of his own presidential possibilities. It was assumed that there would be fireworks when they met. Once again the breath-holders' hopes were dashed. Each man behaved well. The walking stick was never shaken, or even raised.

Still more extraordinary was the meeting after so many years of Old Hickory and that brilliant buffoon Thomas Hart Benton. The last time these two had faced each other, back on the wild frontier, they had had guns in their hands and bitter curses on their lips. Now the newcomer, Jackson, looked around the Senate chamber and spotted the freshman solon Benton at a desk, and went there. Eyes were bulbed, tongues bitten. Fireworks? The Hero bowed politely, Senator Benton rose and bowed back, and they shook hands. The walking stick was not raised, not even shaken. Addressing themselves by their titles of colonel and general, these two chatted pleasantly for a little while, then parted with something like a smile.

From that time on Thomas Hart Benton, though scarcely of a slavish nature, was Andrew Jackson's slave.

It was one of the miracles of American politics—one lion lying down with another.

Benton was never a member of the Kitchen Cabinet. He was not welcome to come and go at the White House any time he pleased. There was certainly nothing sinister about the man; he did all of his fighting out in the open and with conventional weapons, nothing surreptitious. Socially, although they did not avoid one another, the two were not close. Benton made no attempt to cash in on the fact of his early acquaintance with the President. The most he would do, when crowded into a corner, was to remind his opponents with a significant leer that they could be offending "the conqueror of the conquerors of Bonaparte." He was a man who played to win, and that was his trump card.

Neither man ever mentioned the Nashville brawl, at least in the presence of others. Each of them had engaged in more formal, more "correct" combats, and in Missouri, Benton like Jackson had killed his man. Each was a firm believer in the usefulness, the justice, of the code duello; neither would have consented to have his fighting record attributed to youthful exuberance or just plain hotheadedness; and Jackson at least kept on the mantelpiece of the principal parlor in the Hermitage for all to see, the very pistol with which he had killed Charles Dickinson.

Nobody ever brought up the subject before President Jackson, who seemed to have forgotten it, or was trying to. As for Thomas Hart Benton, when as occasionally happened somebody playfully reminded him that he had once engaged in a gun battle with the General, he would shrug, saying something like "Well, which of us didn't, in those days?" and change the subject.

Senator Benton was invited to every White House dinner that he should have been invited to, but the relations between the two, proper in public, in private did not appear to exist. They were co-workers in the cause of the common man; they were sturdy defenders of the Western point of view; but they were not friends.

When Jackson vetoed the Maysville Road bill there were those among his followers who feared that he was changing his course, that he was ceasing to be their companion. Thomas Hart Benton, however, defended him as vigorously as ever.

The Presidents of the United States, thus far, had used the veto privilege gingerly, if at all. Although it was provided for in the Constitution, right there in black and white, the veto, political thinkers tended to think, was somehow a measure of emergency, its use an admission of weakness. They even believed that there might be something shameful about it.

Andrew Jackson did not subscribe to this belief. Whenever he thought that a bill was wrong, he refused to sign it and sent it back to Congress with the reasons for his refusal, as provided in the Constitution. This shocked some congressmen, who believed that the President was overdoing the business, and it gave rise again to the talk—always baseless—that the Hero of New Orleans was somehow working toward a takeover of the legislature by the executive department, that is, a takeover of the government, a military coup.

Jackson also was the first President to use the "pocket veto," a device by means of which the chief executive could kill a bill without committing his reasons to paper: if there were fewer than ten days to go (not counting the Sabbath and national holidays) before Congress had to adjourn, he simply stuck the bill into his pocket and forgot about it. Once again, politicos of that time seemed to think that there was something at least unethical about such a procedure, although many presidents since then have used it without rebuke.

The Maysville Road bill would have authorized Congress to subscribe to some of the stock of the Maysville Road Company, a private concern. The amount of money involved was not large. The principle was.

143

New York State recently had built the Erie Canal, 363 miles long, between Troy and Buffalo, at a cost of $7,500,000. Not only that, but it had also built many feeders to this ditch—the Oswego, Cayuga, Seneca, Chenango, Crooked Lake, and Chemung canals. And the state had paid for them out of its own pocket. The system was a sensational success. In one fell swoop New York had become the gateway to the West, *the* way around the mountains. This enormously increased New York City's importance as a port. It also increased Wall Street's growing lead over Chestnut Street as a financial center.

Of course Pennsylvania tried to emulate this feat. The Chesapeake and Ohio Canal, having to go over so many high places, requiring the construction of so many locks, would be much, much more expensive. The State of Maryland was induced to help, but even that wasn't enough. In the West the newly formed states, poor enough to begin with, went into a frenzy of transportation development. Think big, they were urged, and they did. Michigan, four fifths of it wilderness, and with a population of less than 200,000, blithely contracted for the building of roads and canals calculated to cost something like $8,000,000. Indiana contracted for $20,000,000 worth of improvements: 840 miles of canal, 90 miles of railroad, 335 miles of turnpikes. These, it was hoped, would be paid for by means of bonds sold to foreign investors, especially Englishmen, since nobody in Indiana had money like that. Europeans, however, did not warm to this enticement.

The railroad item is worth noting. It was rare. Railroads were new, and they were noisy, dirty, dangerous. They seemed an unnatural way to transport goods from one place to another, a way that would only be resorted to in an emergency, as a stopgap. The railroad had no future, bankers said. It would never be anything more than an auxiliary, a connecting link between canals and roads.

But, again, who was going to pay for all this? The states

couldn't. Eastern bankers and English financiers alike were leery of it. So the improvers turned to Washington, seeking federal grants.

New York immediately squawked. It had paid for its own canals, and the other states should do the same, it averred. For them to build competing lines at government expense would be grossly unfair. The Southern states agreed, though for a different reason. They hadn't incurred those enormous debts, they pointed out. Let Michigan and Pennsylvania and Indiana scoop their own chestnuts out of the fire.

Pennsylvania, Indiana, Michigan, and the others argued that the country was ridiculously rich anyway just then, with more money coming in than it knew what to do with, so why not? Besides, although these various transportation projects were all within the limits of their separate states, undoubtedly they would when completed carry traffic that would go on to other states and so could be classified as interstate commerce. Wouldn't this put subsidies to such ventures under the aegis of Alexander Hamilton's "implied powers" interpretation of the Constitution?

No, the Jeffersonians cried, it wouldn't. Nothing would. There were no such powers, and never had been.

Here was a crux. With the United States growing by leaps and bounds, the treasury bursting at the seams, men forever setting out upon new commercial ventures, whether or not the federal government could be induced to contribute to the efforts of the individual states might make all the difference in the world.

The Maysville Road bill was not the first piece of such legislation, only the first that happened to reach the President's desk.

The Maysville Road could not, by the most strained definition, be called an interstate thoroughfare. It would be entirely within the boundaries of Kentucky.

Andrew Jackson had no reason to hesitate. Nor did he.

145

True, there were those among his adherents who believed that if only to get votes, if only to keep the Hamiltonians quiet for a little while, he would consent to consider the road necessary for national defense. He *had* once opined that it might be well if the central government supported road and canal projects that would contribute to the national safety. Undoubtedly he had had in memory when he offered this thought the excruciating difficulties he'd encountered when as commander of the Seventh Military District he was trying to pacify the Creeks and later to stop the British. Virtually all military supplies must come from the East, either from New England or the middle states, where the manufactories were. When in the War of 1812 the Royal Navy clamped a blockade upon the entire American coast, they concentrated upon the Southern and Gulf states, which made the supply problem in New Orleans a terrible one. Andrew Jackson unquestionably would have approved the appropriation of federal funds for the improvement of such routes as the old Natchez Trace, little more than a zigzag of tentatively connected Indian trails. In other words, he would have approved of a real military road. The proposed Maysville Road would not be that.

The bill on the desk before him in the White House had another aspect that he might have considered but, perhaps, didn't.

The Maysville Road would run very close to Ashland, Henry Clay's plantation near Lexington. Ashland was a "landlocked" estate; that is, it was not built along a river, as so many of them were—the Hermitage, for instance. Such a road, providing it with an outlet for its products, would greatly increase the value of Ashland. Henry Clay had missed the big job in 1824 and 1828, but nobody doubted that he would be the anti-administration party's nominee again in 1832, which loomed. A "smart" politician could have much hay with this. The thought probably never passed Andrew Jackson's mind. He certainly made no mention of it in the careful, dignified veto message he wrote and sent back with the unsigned Maysville Road bill.

15

THE MAN WHO SAID NO

That swart Olympian, Daniel Webster, had a way with words. Turning a memorable phrase was, to him, as easy as sneezing. Of the Hero he once said, "General Jackson is an honest and upright man. He does what he thinks is right, and does it with all his might." The Archangel himself might veer in his course, as circumstances seemed to suggest. His own district, New England, which had depended upon farming, fishing, and sea carrying, found it impossible after the War of 1812 to renew much of its trade, which had been largely with Great Britain and the British West Indies. The fisheries were resumed, and profitably, but as new lands were opened in the West, and it was learned how exceedingly fertile they were—the wheat yield per acre in Wisconsin, for one example, was thirty times that of stone-studded Connecticut—farming declined in New England.

The blockade had brought about a great shortage of "boughten" objects, manufactured things, and particularly small metal ones like nails and locks and hinges, all of which had come from Great Britain. As a result, many of the money men in the middle states of New York, New Jersey, and Pennsylvania began to establish factories—and to clamor for federal subsidies in the form of high preferential tariffs.

New Englanders, stubbornly striving to revive their farms, their shipbuilding, their foreign trade, were late in getting into the manufacturing business, and in consequence their glorious spokesman in the United States Senate was late in getting to see the manifold blessings for the American people contained in a high import tax schedule. Unabashed, he came around. He who had cried, "Liberty and Union, one and inseparable, now and forever!" cried out now in favor of a system that was splitting the nation right down the middle. Such switches were routine to Daniel Webster.

It was not so, and never could be so, with Andrew Jackson. He had been brought up in the Virginia planter's tradition of indebtedness. He had owed money most of his life. But if there was one thing that he had in his head when they made him President of the United States in 1828, it was that the nation, in order to hold its own among nations of the world, must be able to pay its way.

Jackson was given little credit in his own day for this worthy if old-fashioned idea, and he has been given none since. Yet he clung to it. He made it the theme, the motif, of his administration.

The country had started as a debtor, after assuming all the obligations of the colonies-just-become-states, thus enlarging its own credit, according to a formula set forth by the first Secretary of the Treasury.

When the Federalists, squabbling among themselves, at last had been brushed out of the seats of power, and Thomas Jefferson had taken over the presidency, he and his followers bent every effort to undo this policy of indebtedness, to reverse this money outflow. "It is incumbent on every generation to pay its own debts as it goes—a principle which, if acted on, would save one half the wars of the world," Jefferson had written. Also: "The principle of spending money to be paid by posterity, under the name of funding, is but swindling futurity on a large scale."

The new democrats had just begun to get the national

finances back on an even keel, by the simple process of refusing to spend money that they didn't have, when their labors were interrupted by an offer from the First Consul of France, Bonaparte, who proposed to sell the entire territory of Louisiana for fourteen million dollars. This offer had been entirely unexpected. The nation didn't have that much money, and as the revered father of strict constructionism, Thomas Jefferson at first could not conceive of pledging it to such a sum when the Constitution clearly did not authorize the purchase of territory. That would be to lean upon Alexander Hamilton's doctrine of implied powers, anathema to Jeffersonians.

President Jefferson had hesitated, almost panicked. He had suggested that the Constitution be amended, but there was no time for such a procedure. The erratic and unpredictable First Consul, American ambassadors in Paris wrote, already was thinking of withdrawing his offer, which was simply too good to let go. So Thomas Jefferson sighed, and he wrote to Robert Livingston and James Monroe to go ahead with the biggest real estate deal in history, which they did.

This set the democrats back a bit, but they persisted, and in time they succeeded in getting the country solvent again.

Then came the War of 1812, and the nation was plunged into debt once more, so that it was necessary to revive, under suitable restrictions, the Bank of the United States. And the Virginia Dynasts had to start all over again.

This effort Andrew Jackson proposed to complete. The BUS in his eyes had outlived its usefulness, if it ever had any, and the taxpayers must be spared those terrible interest charges.

This determination surely had something to do with his introduction into government of what an ungrateful posterity has been pleased to call the Spoils System. To him it was largely a way of weeding out the grafters, the inefficient; in other words, it was a way of cutting expenses.

"If a national debt is considered a national blessing, then

149

we can get on by borrowing," Andrew Jackson had written. "But as I believe it is a national curse, my vow shall be to pay the national debt."

This determination too must have been back of his veto of the Maysville Road bill, which carried with it a warning that he would oppose all other attempts to appropriate federal funds for intrastate projects.

It undoubtedly was the root cause of his decision to change his mind about not running again and to announce, formally, from the White House, January 22, 1831, that he would be a candidate for President in 1832.

Running again was his duty, obviously. The national debt had been whittled down to a mere seven million, and Jackson in a report to Congress reckoned that it would be wiped out by the end of 1833—but only, of course, if he was there to supervise the job. He had started it; he must finish it. So he would run again.

The announcement, made quietly and without comment, was a bombshell for those who were playing the political game. It reshook all their plans about the succession, the most exciting sport in Washington. Previously all calculations had been based upon a four-year Jackson presidency. Now it seemed that with the man's immense popularity, which seemed to grow greater all the time, he could have a second term any time he asked for it.

Calhoun's stock already was falling. When he lost Pennsylvania to Jackson in the 1828 caucus he had nothing but the South to fall back upon, and now he was growing more and more Southern every day, vociferously opposing the tariff, which once he had seemed to support, and talking a great deal, ominously, about states' rights. Yet Jackson was a Southerner too.

John Quincy Adams was still in the ring, still shadowboxing, but even in the House, where he was highly regarded, men muttered that he could never live down his Federalist past.

Anyway—it was a family propensity—he had made too many enemies.

Julia Chinn, the mulatto who had lived so long with Colonel Johnson, he of the red waistcoats, was dead now, and southerners were willing to forget about what were called the colonel's "domestic conditions." He could still be thought in the running, but not, of course, against Andrew Jackson.

Winfield Scott remained a conspicuous figure, if only because he had grown so fat. As a presidential possibility he had two big assets: an impressive appearance and a distinguished military career. On both of these, however, he was outmatched by Andrew Jackson.

To be sure, there was still—there always was—Henry Clay.

The Mill Boy of the Slashes was bringing out crowds as never before. Speaker of the House, then Secretary of State, now a senator, he was called, not idly, the Great Compromiser. He really thought that he could get the government out of just about any jam that less skillful men might have got it into, and he said so, forcefully. His American System was proving itself, he believed. The Eastern manufacturers were interested. As for the Bank of the United States, Clay strongly favored it, considering it an integral part of the American System, which was Hamilton's old, discredited rich-men's-government yanked from out of its dusty corner, brushed off, propped up. The Bank's charter would not run out until 1836, but once Andrew Jackson had declared his intention of running for reelection the Great Compromiser declared that application should be made for a new charter—right away. They had the votes; they could get the grant. And on the eve of a presidential election the Hero, no matter what he'd said in his message to Congress, no matter what Benton declared in his name from the floor of the Senate, would never dare to veto it.

"If Jackson should veto," Clay told Nicholas Biddle, "I'll veto Jackson!"

Those were strong words.

For some time John C. Calhoun kept hoping to win the heir-apparency nod, his principal rival here being Martin Van Buren, who was now in England. These hopes were burst when "the cast-iron man" allowed himself to be drawn into an argument with his chief, even before Jackson's announcement that he would run again.

Some helpful friends showed Jackson a letter written by a member of the War of 1812 cabinet in which it was asserted that the Secretary of War, Calhoun, now Vice President, had cast doubts upon the legality of General Jackson's invasion of Florida. This of course the Secretary had every right to do, and he was not alone in questioning the propriety of that invasion.

President Jackson, furious—taking it, as he took everything, personally—wrote to his own Vice President demanding an explanation. Calhoun should have told him, politely of course, to go to hell. What went on at cabinet meetings was the members' own business. They were not responsible to anybody, not even to the President—and Jackson of course had not been President at that time, only a general in the field—for their opinions or their remarks.

This took place before Jackson had declared his intention of serving the nation for four more years, however, and Calhoun was still hopeful of becoming the next occupant of the White House. He answered at great length, but cloudily. He almost cringed. Obviously the man was frightened. It cannot be thought that he feared for his life, despite the sternness of the President's letter. For the President of the United States to call out the Vice President—that is, challenge him to a duel—was unthinkable. No, it was the succession that Calhoun was thinking of.

The President wrote again, and he was curt, asking for an explanation of that long, rambling letter, and the best the cowed Calhoun could do was answer with an even longer, even more rambling letter, which cleared up nothing.

The President then wrote that this correspondence should be considered closed, and he never spoke to John C. Calhoun again.

It could be that the famous intellect had relaxed its grip upon Calhoun for a little while at just this time. Otherwise, it is hard to explain why he then did two supremely foolish things.

He published the correspondence with President Jackson, a correspondence that by anybody's standards, North or South, democratic or aristocratic, made Calhoun look weak and obsequious. And he set about blocking ratification of Martin Van Buren's appointment as ambassador to Great Britain.

Sweet Sandy Whiskers had not waited for that ratification, which seemed certain. He and his chirpy secretary Washington Irving were scoring a great success in London, where they had settled down for what looked like a long stay.

The House of Representatives has nothing to say about presidential appointments to foreign posts. This privilege is reserved for the United States Senate. Jackson's majority in the Senate was slight but usually firm, but it could be that at this time the senators were smarting under the slap of presidential vetoes and so were liable to listen to urgings that they apply a veto of their own. Calhoun as Vice President was presiding officer of the Senate without a vote, except in the case of a tie, but he was not above quitting his seat to go down on the floor and cajole individual members. His influence in the chamber was strong. He contrived to rig a tie vote, and with undisguised glee, on a bitter cold night late in January of 1832, he voted against ratification of Van Buren.

"It will kill him, sir, kill him!" Thomas Hart Benton overheard the Vice President tell a friend, immediately after the vote. "He will never kick, sir, never kick!"

As so often, Mr. Calhoun was wrong. The refusal to ratify was obviously a mean-spirited political trick designed to embar-

153

rass the Wizard of Old Kinderhook, and it resulted in a welling up of sympathy for the smart little man, who was about to come home. Also, it was a deliberate punch in Andrew Jackson's nose, and Jackson was not a man to ignore such punches.

Calhoun, whose term was about to expire, had made it certain who the next Vice President would be—unless, of course, Henry Clay won.

Jackson himself, though not noted for his political acumen, saw this. But Jackson was much more interested in the war against the Bank of the United States. Marty Van, back in New York, refrained at first from hurrying to Washington, a move that could have been interpreted as a sign of weakness, of lack of confidence, but he soon got a summons, and went to the White House, which he reached at midnight.

The President, bolstered up, looked rather more than half dead. He seemed to be coughing his life away. He had been taking massive doses of calomel for his diarrhea, and was so weak that he could scarcely reach a hand to this helpful old friend.

"The Bank is trying to kill me," he told Marty Van—and he meant this literally—"but *I will kill it!*"

Biddle had decided to take Henry Clay's advice. His lobbyists, together with the senators and representatives who were his friends—Clay, Webster, John Quincy Adams, George McDuffie, Horace Binney, Edward Everett, a formidable team—told him that a renewal application could be adopted at this time, and after he had taken the field in person, coming down from Philadelphia, he agreed with them. He knew that the voting margin would be small in both houses, but he believed that Henry Clay was right when he declared that the Hero of New Orleans would not dare to veto a bank charter renewal bill on the eve of a presidential election. On January 9, 1832, Biddle formally applied for a renewal of the charter for twenty years.

Benton, who had been expecting this, had prepared many

obstructionist measures, but they were overridden. He even had difficulty getting the floor, and when at last he did, on February 2, he explained at length his reasons for opposing a recharter: "I look upon the Bank as an institution too great and powerful to be tolerated in a Government of free and equal laws. . . . It tends to aggravate the inequality of fortunes; to make the rich richer, and the poor poorer; to multiply nabobs and paupers . . . on account of the exclusive privileges, and anti-republican monopoly, which it gives to stockholders." The speech was simpler and more free of fustian than usual. That it changed a single vote in Congress is to be doubted, but it had a tremendous effect outside, where it was much published and discussed.

Nevertheless, on June 11 the Senate passed the renewal bill 28 to 20. On July 3 the House passed it 107 to 86.

On July 10 Andrew Jackson vetoed it.

16

THE EDGE OF CHAOS

Randolph of Roanoke was abusive, abrasive, a very volcano of vituperation, a man who seemed to carry lemon juice in his mouth instead of spit. But he had the answers to almost everything, and if those answers often were irreverent they could be thought-provoking too, as when Randolph was chided by a Northerner who suggested that he might bend his insistence upon states' rights to include a few exceptions, and he retorted, "Asking one of the States to surrender part of her sovereignty is like asking a lady to surrender part of her chastity."

The Northerner was silenced. Others weren't. The beginnings of that great rift that was to be ended only by the costliest war the world had ever known already were plain upon the corpus of government. However, there were many who wouldn't look upon them, for fear of seeing something unpleasant.

Calhoun did not invent nullification, although he liked to have it thought that he did. He did not even call it that, preferring "state interposition" or "the veto." A mention of "secession" would have caused him to scream. The whole idea of the "state interposition" movement, he used to announce, was to keep the union together, not to tear it apart.

Here is the way Calhoun reasoned: Sovereignty, the ultimate source of power, lies in the states—in the states, that is, considered as separate political communities. These separate communities, or peoples, through their ratifying conventions had authorized the Constitution and the federal government. That is, the peoples were "principals," in legal terminology, while the federal government was their "agent." The Constitution was a "compact" containing instructions within which the agent was to operate. This was perfectly clear to him, and he couldn't see why it was not clear to everybody else.

Robert J. Turnbull, another South Carolinian, is generally credited with originating nullification, at least under that name, for he like the other Nullies always attributed the movement to the Kentucky and Virginia resolutions of 1798, the former written by Thomas Jefferson, the latter by James Madison, although neither of these statesmen acknowledged his authorship.

Calhoun did not even sound the first clarion. This was done by Dr. Thomas Cooper, president of South Carolina College, in the summer of 1827, at Columbia.

Jefferson himself had said of Dr. Cooper, "He is acknowledged, by every enlightened man who knows him, to be the greatest man in America in the powers of his mind and in acquired information." The more censorious John Quincy Adams had found him "a learned, ingenious, scientific, and talented mad-cap."

What Dr. Cooper said at that public meeting was: "We shall, ere long, be compelled to calculate the value of our Union; and to inquire of what use to us is this most unequal alliance by which the South has always been the loser and the North the gainer? . . . The question, however, is fast approaching the alternative, submission or separation."

If that wasn't a call to get out, what was it?

Not long after Dr. Cooper's flaming speech, but *just* after the election of Andrew Jackson, the South Carolina legislature adopted a statement that soon came to be known as the "Exposition" of the nullification movement. Calhoun himself had written it, but had not yet acknowledged it. He, like so many other

157

South Carolina leaders, looked upon the Exposition not as an irreversible declaration of intentions but rather as a bare toe stuck into the water of a swimming hole for the purpose of determining its temperature.

The Exposition, no masterpiece of reason, set forth, as had both the Kentucky and Virginia resolutions, that when any state considered any act of the federal Congress to be a breach of that "compact," the Constitution, it could, whether by convention or by legislation, call upon Congress to repeal it, and if Congress should refuse to do this, the state could declare that statute null and void, acting, as we should say now, unilaterally. Just what would happen after that was anybody's guess. The Exposition, wisely perhaps, did not dip into the future.

It was stipulated that a balky state, before it took this action, would invite other states to join it. No mention, however, was made of the fact that the Virginia and Kentucky resolutions had been monumental flops. Each was passed in its state legislature by a majority vote, but each obviously depended upon the cooperation or at least the sympathy of that state's neighbors, and when each was sent by the governor to the governors of all the other states the response, when there was any response at all, was a flat no.

That would seem to dispose of the Kentucky and Virginia resolutions as guideposts. Yet the Nullies persisted. Although the United States Constitution plainly states, "This Constitution and the laws made in pursuance thereof shall be the supreme law of the land, anything in the constitution or laws of any state to the contrary notwithstanding," still the Nullies induced the legislature of South Carolina to demand that everybody elected to a state office should be made to take this oath: "I, A.B., do solemnly swear, or affirm, that I will be faithful and true allegiance bear to the state of South Carolina; and that I will support and maintain, to the utmost of my ability, the laws and constitution of this state and the United States; so help me God." There was even a movement to require all of those already in office to take this oath, on pain of eviction. It lost by a whisker.

It must be remembered that South Carolina was the most "aristocratic" of the states, politically speaking. It still subscribed to the stake-in-society theory of suffrage: those who have it should say what's to be done with it. A handful of men, because of their families, controlled South Carolina, and they meant to keep it that way. Most of the states, during or immediately after the Revolution, adopted suffrage standards that were higher than they had been while England was in control, a curious thing to do in the circumstances. These states were gradually relaxing their suffrage laws, lowering their standards, and admitting into a share of the government all but out-and-out paupers, of which there were very few anyway. The western states, as one by one they came into the Union, displayed a tendency to favor the so-called common man, the poor man, who in fact *was* common in those parts. But not South Carolina! It clung to its Toryism, a standpat.

South Carolina, despite this seeming backwardness, aspired to the leadership of the South that Virginia lately had lost. It would be the bellwether.

Was the new President really a Southerner? South Carolina was among the first to ask this question. He owned slaves, he raised racehorses, he had the rank of major general, so he must be a gentleman. But was he, truly, a Southerner? Did he *think* as a Southerner? There were those in Charleston who doubted it.

In the matter of the Indians, this new President certainly seemed to favor states' rights over those of the federal government, and whether or not he had ever said "John Marshall has made his decision—now let him enforce it," he certainly had *acted* that way. But how did he stand on the tariff? Here, the Nullies insisted, was the nut of the whole matter. Here was

159

the point that must be settled before anything else could be done, for the very future of the United States hung upon it.

At the end of the War of 1812 the United States, with a population of barely nine million, its trade moribund, was $130,000,000 in debt. It was then that there began, in the Northern states, the digging-in of manufacturers, which it was hoped would become a permanent part of the regional scene. Men who had begun to make things, and to sell them, understandably tried to kill off or at least to cripple competition from abroad, and the quickest, cleanest, most convenient way to do it was by getting the federal government to raise the tax on imports. The tax, of course, raised the price of these products in the United States, and American manufacturers raised *their* prices high enough so as just to outsell the imports. Thus, the manufacturers made a much bigger profit, and were able to sink this extra money into new factories, for the products of which they demanded further "protection" in the form of tariff rises.

All of this greatly raised the cost of living, a condition offset, in the Northern states, at least to some extent, by the wages paid at the new factories. But the South did not get any of those new factories, didn't want any of them, and was, it would seem, irrevocably agrarian. Why then should the South be taxed so that Northern manufacturers could make more money?

The tariff on imports had been first imposed, its originator Alexander Hamilton explained, because the federal government had needed this revenue. But the federal government no longer needed revenue. In fact, what with the rapid reduction of its debt, the sale of public lands in the West, and the general prosperity of the country, the federal government would soon have more money than it knew what to do with, and already the national legislators were considering plans for splitting the surplus with the states. Yet those Yankees kept clamoring for higher tariff rates. Why?

The South depended in large part upon cotton, and because

the British naval blockade in the late war had brought about the opening of new cotton fields, especially in Egypt and India, and also because still other new cotton fields had been opened in the United States west of the mountains, where the rich Black Belt of Alabama-Mississippi-Louisiana was being exploited to the full, the price of cotton in the world market was steadily going down. In 1818, just after the war, cotton had wholesaled at 31¢ a pound; in 1821 this was 14¢; in 1826 it was 10¢. Now, in 1831, it was down to 8¢ a pound, and what was the federal government doing about that?

The Nullies were not nearsighted. They saw clearly enough the implications of protectionism and what it would lead to. Every session of Congress became a logrolling contest. A manufacturer who wanted the tariff on his product upped would combine with another manufacturer who wanted the same thing for his product, and between them, and with the help of a few others in a similar position, they got what they wanted for their "infant industries." Their districts got factories and smoke and soot, higher wages, more jobs, and millionaires' mansions, but the South got nothing but bigger bills for the goods it had to buy. This vicious circle would enlarge itself, always at the expense of the farmer. It fed upon its own fat. It was self-perpetuating.

Henry Clay was to the American System what John C. Calhoun was to Nullification, not its inventor but surely the highest of its high priests. Clay could explain, glibly enough, that the American System *did* benefit the American farmer, somehow, but the planter of the South, regarding eight-cent cotton and the enormously increased cost of his "boughten" objects, had difficulty agreeing. The process must be stopped—and sharply, immediately. Otherwise, the South soon would become no more than a backyard, a dumping ground for unwanted trash; the Southerner would become a servant—nay, a slave—of the moneyed Northerner.

ANDREW JACKSON, HERO

Upon this much virtually all South Carolinians were agreed, but they were not agreed on Nullification as the remedy.

The Nullies were no fly-by-nights. Their resentment was honest, it was logical, it was deep-seated. They were not so many crackpots, firebrands, carried away by the excitement of the moment. They had reasons for their resolution. They numbered in their ranks the Governor of South Carolina and both senators, and they commanded as well a majority, if a slim one, of the legislature. They were some of the wealthiest men and some of the most intelligent in the South.

But they had opponents. These the Nullies labeled Submission Men—also cowards, recreants, tories, etc. The Submission Men called themselves Unionists, designating the State Rights Association as "Jacobinical" and "a clear case of *imperium in imperio.*" But the Nullies went right on purchasing arms, drilling volunteer companies, making ready, it would seem, not for mere riots but for war.

Although large numbers of Southerners watched the development of the Nullification movement, wary about committing themselves, in South Carolina everybody had to be on one side or the other, nobody being allowed to remain in what was then called a state of inbetweenity. The Submission Men insisted that Nullification, the right to abrogate any law passed by the federal government, was "anarchy reduced to system." The Nullies, on the other hand, cried out that to continue to allow the Yankees to take over the economy would be, purely and simply, suicide.

Andrew Jackson, though he was no more sure of his birthplace than we are today, liked to refer to himself as "a son of South Carolina." Surely he was no man to run away from a misunderstanding. In this case, however, he decided to try a little quiet conciliation first. His agent in this attempt was an amateur botanist named Joel Poinsett, a South Carolinian of impeccable ancestry, powerful family connections, and great personal charm. Poinsett was the first American statesman to have a flower named after him—the poinsettia, cuttings of which he brought from Mexico, where he had been the U.S. ambassador—but he was no shrinking violet. For all his celebrated elegance, he knew the rough-and-tumble of politics, and was never afraid to get his knuckles skinned. He and President Jackson were the closest of friends. Jackson, of course, was obliged to remain in Washington during the crisis. Poinsett directed Union activities in the field.

Thomas Jefferson's birthday, April 13—he had been dead four years—was to be celebrated in 1830 with a bang-up banquet at Brown's Indian Queen Hotel in Washington, a banquet both the President and the Vice President had promised to attend. Twenty-four "regular" toasts were scheduled, and of course as many "volunteer" toasts would follow as circumstances might suggest. There was much buzz about the presidential acceptance. He seldom did consent to go to affairs like this. Did that mean he would use the occasion to tell the world where he stood on the matter of Nullification? It did.

A toast did not mean a drink, necessarily. It meant a short speech, and it was to be acknowledged, ordinarily, by murmured hear-hear's, little more. But there had to be a drink somewhere, and the President, when he rose in his place, looking taller and more the death's-head than ever, had a glass in his hand. With the other hand palm up he signaled for a general standing.

"Our Federal Union—it must be preserved!"

The applause was deafening. The Hero, it was agreed, had given his answer.

Jackson was a hard act to follow. Calhoun, when he rose in his place, faltered. "The Union—next to our Liberty most dear." That might be all right, so far, though it called for some thinking out, but the Vice President was not prepared to let well enough alone, and he plugged on. "May we all remember that it can only be preserved by respecting the rights of the

163

States and distributing equally the benefit and burthen of the Union." He did not get much applause.

Nevertheless, the ladies of South Carolina went on sewing blue cockades, the emblem of state sovereignty. The men of South Carolina, many of them anyway, went on writing letters of encouragement to John C. Calhoun, in many cases addressing them to "President of the Confederated States of America."

So they really wanted a fight?

"In forty days I can have within the limits of South Carolina fifty thousand men, and in forty days more another fifty thousand," Jackson wrote to Joel Poinsett. He gave him permission to publish this letter.

To a South Carolina congressman who was about to go home the President said, "Tell them from me that they can talk and write resolutions and print threats to their hearts' content. But if one drop of blood be shed there in defiance of the laws of the United States, I will hang the first man of them I can get my hands on to the first tree I can find."

Robert Y. Hayne, he who had been Daniel Webster's opponent in the week-long "debate" about union, was quitting the Senate and about to go back to South Carolina to become that state's governor. He was a red-hot Nullificationist. He'd heard about the President's threat. "D'ye think he means it?" he asked Thomas Hart Benton.

"I tell you, when Jackson begins to talk about hanging," Benton replied, "they can begin to look for the ropes."

Hayne went home anyway. In the course of the game of political musical chairs they were playing there his place in the Senate was to be taken by John C. Calhoun, who, knowing now that he would not again be named Vice President, was about to resign.

The tariff was to cause the Civil War—not slavery, which was an afterthought complicated by the Mexican War and the acquisition of new land in the West. Greedy men wear blinders.

Gain is their god; they see nothing else. The manufacturers had plans to push through Congress an even higher tariff law, and the Nullies of South Carolina could see only one way to stop it.

On November 19, 1832, at Columbia, a special state convention voted 136 to 26 to declare the federal tariff acts "null, void, and no law, nor binding upon this State, its officers or citizens." No duties were to be collected after February 1, 1833. The legislature was to affirm this resolution and pass laws to enforce it. This the legislature did.

Here was deliberate, open defiance of the federal government. Jackson ceased his bluster, but did not cease his preparations to meet the threat. He alerted the customs officials at Charleston, the only port of entry in South Carolina, and warned them that they should never, no matter what the force brought against them, relinquish their duties. He ordered General Scott to bring a great part of his total force into North Carolina and Virginia, though they were not to step over the line into South Carolina unless and until he personally ordered them to. He applied to Congress for a law that would specifically give him leave to use whatever military measures he saw fit in this emergency. He did not need such a law—he knew that—but it would strengthen his hand and might serve to abash the Nullies.

He issued a proclamation. There was no rant in the proclamation, no rodomontade. It was simple.

"I consider the power to annul a law of the United States, assumed by one State, incompatible with the existence of the Union, contradicted expressly by the letter of the Constitution, unauthorized by its spirit, inconsistent with every principle on which it was founded, and destructive of the great object for which it was formed."

The 1832 tariff bill had established very low duties on silks, which the country didn't produce anyway, and it specified no duties at all on coffee or tea, which the country did not produce, either. These were gestures, intended to divert the anti-tariff men's attention from the rates on manufactured articles, the rates that really counted; *they* averaged, at that time, about 33 percent.

The Nullies had announced that they would settle for nothing less than a horizontal level of reduction to 15 or 20 percent.

Trouble was due when the new Congress sat. The day when South Carolina's nullification ordinance would go into effect, February 1, was fast approaching.

Jackson was granted his extraordinary military powers, in a measure known officially as the Wilkins bill, unofficially as the force bill, though the Nullies inclined to call it "a bill to dissolve the Union."

The country held its breath.

The handful of men who held the reins in Charleston had by this time created Robert Y. Hayne governor (they did have elections in South Carolina, but these didn't mean anything) and had elected John C. Calhoun, who had resigned as Vice President, United States Senator. Calhoun thereupon had returned to Washington.

Calhoun's trip was fraught with peril, for rumors that he would be shot somewhere on the way were thick. Even after he had arrived intact he wasn't safe. Many men said, and believed, that President Jackson would seize him and hang him. President Jackson didn't.

Calhoun took his place to be sworn in before the whole Senate. He was calm and dignified, and the dignity was natural, not theatrical, not show-off. *Could* he swear to uphold the Constitution of the United States, although only a few days ago he had taken the South Carolina oath, which placed state allegiance first? He could, and he did. Then he stepped down to the floor, and sought out Henry Clay.

A congressman named Verplanck, a New Yorker, together with the Secretary of the Treasury, McLane, both protectionists, had concocted a new tariff bill, which was meant to be a compromise, although most certainly it would not satisfy the Nullies. It would have reduced federal revenues by about thirteen million dollars, giving the manufacturers pretty much the same detailed protection that the tariff bill of 1816 had given them. It would thus destroy all of the protectionist gains of 1820, 1824, 1828, and 1830. But obviously it would not last.

Now suddenly the Great Compromiser came out with a brand-new bill, one that he himself had just written. It was extremely complicated, designed, it would seem, to confuse all possible opponents, and in this it could serve as a prototype, because all subsequent tariff bills have been characterized by mosquitolike swarms of figures clearly calculated to discombobulate the inattentive.

Clay's bill afforded the full 1832 protection for the next nine years—Clay himself, privately, did not think that it would last as long as that—while on January 1, 1834, there would be a cut of 10 percent in rates in excess of 20 percent, another 10 percent cut January 1, 1836, 10 percent more January 1, 1838, and again January 1, 1840, by which time four tenths of the excess over 20 percent would be gone. On January 1, 1842, one half of the remaining excess would be cut out, and July 1, 1842, the rest would be cut out, leaving a uniform 20 percent.

This masterpiece of ratiocination, or whatever it was, was introduced into the House of Representatives, where all revenue bills must originate. Clay himself was a senator now, but he had been Speaker of the House for many years and was its most accomplished and ingenious legislative prestidigitator. Through a miracle of hanky-panky that political historians even today look back upon with awe, he managed to get the bill introduced into the House, bumping, as we would say today, the Verplanck bill.

A roar of rage rose from the Nullies, who quite properly came to the conclusion that a trick was being played on them. Then John C. Calhoun, their own god, their adored leader, stepped forward—and *endorsed* the Clay bill. No one will ever be able to explain why he did this, unless it was as a result of some deal with Clay about the next presidential nomination. Anyway, he did, and the Clay bill, mysterious though it was, was pushed through the House and then the Senate, and signed by Andrew Jackson.

The crisis was ended. Civil war had been averted on the very eve of the day that South Carolina's nullification ordinance was to have gone into effect. General Scott was ordered to recall his men. Customs officials at Charleston were notified that there would be no pause in business.

The nullification ordinance was repealed by the South Carolina legislature March 15, 1833, Jackson's sixty-sixth birthday anniversary.

So the conqueror of the conquerors of Bonaparte had done it again. For a second time he had saved his country.

17

DIRTY WORK
ON THE NIAGARA

There was a man in Batavia, New York, who was a mason and a Mason. William Morgan had a wife and two children, and they had recently come up from Culpepper County, Virginia. He was light-complected, of medium height and build, and about forty-five years old. He was also quarrelsome, and he became the central figure in the nation's first great murder mystery.

Morgan did claim to have been at one time a captain in the U.S. Army, and he said that he had served under Andrew Jackson at New Orleans. But that meant little. Every other ablebodied man you met in those days would tell you, after he'd had a few drinks, that he had served under Jackson at New Orleans. It is certain that Jackson himself never heard of William Morgan, even after his body was found. Or *was* it his body? We will never know. In any event, the scandal resulted in the formation of the first real third party in the United States.

Morgan was not making money as a mason, so he thought that he might turn a dirty dollar as a Mason. He was a thirddegree man. He declared that Freemasonry was wicked, and he proposed to expose it. He had written a book spreading on paper all of its secrets, and the book was about to be published. William Morgan said so, often. He said it in the presence of others.

Freemasonry had existed in this country since colonial times, but it was viewed with suspicion by many. All those secret signs, secret handshakes, passwords, unspeakable ceremonies in unsavory places! In time a rash of fraternal organizations was to break out upon the face of the nation, and their curious names and bargain-basement insurance plans and top-heavily entitled officers, not to mention their outlandish costumes, would make the whole business seem rather silly, a small boy's game. But it did not seem silly to the residents of western New York State in 1826. It seemed very sinister indeed, dark and dangerous.

William Morgan should have kept his mouth shut. He was arrested on September 11 on a charge of stealing a shirt and necktie, and was taken to Canandaigua, the seat of Ontario County, where he made good with cash. However, he was immediately arrested again, this time because he owed $2.69 to somebody. He asked to be allowed to go home, offering to leave his coat as security, having no money left in his pocket. This offer was refused, and he spent the night in the county jail, and all the next day too. Late in the afternoon of September 12, as darkness was gathering, he was released, and he was met at the jail door by three men who hustled him into a closed carriage, which, with curtains drawn tight, started west in the direction of Fort Niagara. That was the last ever seen of William Morgan.

The hullabaloo was earsplitting. Men, all Masons, were arrested, but because you can't have a murder charge unless there is a *corpus delicti*, a body, they were allowed to plead guilty to lesser charges and were fined. The fines were immediately forthcoming from some mysterious source. What was *not* forthcoming was an explanation of what had happened to Morgan.

The Masons themselves were doggedly silent. Most of the others asserted, on no authority at all, that Morgan had been driven to Fort Niagara, and there questioned, perhaps tortured, before being strangled, weighted, and dumped into

Lake Ontario. Still others, however, declared that Morgan had been turned loose in Canada, where he was making a living as a bricklayer, and the Governor of New York was persuaded to write to the governors of Lower Canada at Quebec, and Upper Canada, at York, asking if they or any of their constituents had seen such a person in those parts. The answer in each case was negative.

Western New York, "the Burned-Over District," long had been a place for splinter religions, cults, and the hailing of new messiahs. This time, with Anti-Masonry, it outdid itself. It produced a new political party.

Among the first to see the political possibilities in this scandal were Thurlow Weed, a saturnine editor from Albany, and William Henry Seward, a young Auburn lawyer. Politics, they say, makes strange bedfellows. That Seward and Weed ever actually slept together is to be doubted; they were not even close friends; but the Morgan case brought them together, for each had been looking for a path to power that would not involve taking orders from the Albany Regency.

Other than a wish for a new and independent party, these two men had little in common. They did not even look alike, Seward being smallish, earnest, outgoing of manner, talkative, and bright, while Weed was glum, grim, and laconic. Seward strove to be a statesman. He could be portentious of speech and long-winded. He was to become governor of New York, a United States senator, a contender for the Republican nomination for President (he beat out Lincoln in the early ballots at Springfield), and for eight years one of the nation's most distinguished Secretaries of State. He liked to do things in a big way. For example, he bought Alaska for us, something that seemed rash to many Americans at the time: "Seward's Icebox," the new territory was called.

Thurlow Weed, on the other hand, was a master of small detail. He was a compromiser, an arranger of deals, one who

171

whispered in doorways, who avoided the light, preferring rather to lurk in shadow. He was not a brilliant writer, but he had just hired one, a fussy, nearsighted, eccentric young man named Horace Greeley, who could also be rated as one of the fathers of the Whig party, one of the grandfathers of the Republican party. Weed dealt for the most part, and in a large cloudy way, with cloudy large issues, but he was not unaware of the importance in practical politics of the ridiculous. It was he who broke the great patched-pants story when a man he didn't like, a Regency stalwart, William Learned Marcy, was running for governor.

Marcy had an excellent record as a justice of the state supreme court, but Weed, after poring over many old records, came up with the startling fact that once, while on circuit, the judge had turned in an expense account that included a charge of 50¢ "for mending my pantaloons." The editor of the powerful *Evening Journal* made a big thing of this. Here was a jurist, he thundered, who though paid "the princely sum" of two thousand dollars a year, had the temerity to gouge half a dollar out of the long-suffering State of New York for a patch on his pants. Now what did the voters think of *that*? Was *that* the kind of man they would like to see as governor? There was no hint of corruption, but jokes about "the patch in Marcy's pants," many of them ribald, fairly rocked the Empire State all through that bitter campaign. Marcy won, and he was to make an excellent governor, as he had made an excellent state supreme court justice and an excellent United States senator (despite the "to the victor belongs the spoils" speech), but he was never allowed to forget that expense account. That was the way Thurlow Weed played the game.

The Anti-Mason idea caught on fast, and soon after Weed and the others started to work there were state committees in Pennsylvania, Vermont, Ohio, New Jersey, and of course New York. The New England states had begun to come in. The South, however, never did cotton to it.

172

DIRTY WORK ON THE NIAGARA

Here was the first American third party, the first independent "nuisance" party. *The* party, Jefferson's creation, on paper
was still but one, but in fact, and recently in name as well,
it had become two—not two factions of the same machine but
two separate machines. The Democratic Republicans, Jackson's
followers, were the regulars. They were orthodox; but the splinter
scrapings, the disagree-ers, brought together and held together
by Henry Clay, had lately taken to calling themselves National
Republicans, and they were to all intents and purposes an opposition party.

The new third group lacked two important things: a positive
reason for existing, as distinguished from the purely negative
aim of doing away with Freemasonry in the United States, and
a leader of national stature—that is, a presidential possibility.

Taking the anti-administration side, these Johnny-come-
latelies raked together everything that could be considered
moot. They knew that interest in the murder of William Morgan—if there had been a murder—couldn't last forever, although it was still, of course, a vote-getting scandal in western
New York State. When on October 7, 1827, a badly decom-
posed male body was washed ashore on one of the lower banks
of Oak Orchard Creek, near where it empties into Lake Ontario,
some friends, themselves Masons, hurried to Thurlow Weed
with news of the find. But, they warned, it might not be William
Morgan.

"It'll be a good enough Morgan until after the election,"
Weed retorted, and he gave American politics a sprightly and
very useful phrase. "A good enough Morgan" passed into the
language. For the rest of his life, Weed was to protest that what
he had really told his Masonic friends was "a good enough
Morgan until you bring back the one you carried off," but
nobody paid any attention to him. Weed was to be haunted
by "a good enough Morgan" as William L. Marcy had been
haunted by that patch in his gubernatorial pants.

As for a leader, the natural person to look to was Henry

173

Clay, but Clay, unfortunately, was a high-degree Mason.

Neither Seward nor Weed could be considered. One was much too young, still in his twenties, while the other was not candidate material, being a poor public speaker, a nonlawyer, a behind-the-scenes worker, and no man to carry the party banner.

Andrew Jackson himself was a high-ranking Mason, and so was the governor of New York, DeWitt Clinton, who had sent out the alarm for William Morgan. Lewis Cass, who had a high reputation because of his record as governor of the great Northwest Territory, was, alas, another thirty-third degree Mason, as, come to think of it, George Washington too had been. John Quincy Adams answered the Weed-Seward letter of inquiry with characteristic straightforwardness: "I state that I am not, never have been, and never shall be, a Freemason." But Adams didn't count any longer.

The man they did get to accept the nomination, Supreme Court Justice William Wirt, had once been a Mason, though he had not risen high in the order. He agreed to run only if the Anti-Masons agreed not to press Anti-Masonry, the only issue they had.

All the same, this third party made great changes in American political procedure. They gave us the national convention. In Baltimore's Athenaeum (it stood at the southwest corner of St. Paul and Lexington streets), September 26, 1831, they assembled ninety-six delegates from New York, Pennsylvania, Massachusetts, Connecticut, Rhode Island, Vermont, New Jersey, Delaware, Maryland, and Ohio. This group, before duly nominating William Wirt, established several important precedents. It adopted, from state conventions that had taken place previously, the chairman pro tempore, the permanent chairman, and several vice presidents for honorary purposes. It promulgated the first national Address to the People, which was to become the party platform. It applied on a national scale the appointment

174

of delegates according to the electoral strength of the basic unit, in this case the state. It introduced the roll call of delegates by states, the rules committee, the order-of-business committee, the conduct of business through the committee system, and, most important of all, the resort to the nominating convention for selecting its presidential ticket.

"You know I never despair," President Jackson once said to Marty Van. "I have confidence in the virtue and good sense of the people."

The people reciprocated this.

The Hero worked very hard over his messages to Congress. He did not write them, but he picked good men to do the job each time, and he supervised each speech, reading the result over and over, calling for small changes, until he got exactly what he had wanted.

None of these messages raised quite the storm of abuse that the one of July 20, 1832, vetoing the Bank renewal bill, had done. This message had been written by some of the best men in the business—Kendall, Taney, Donelson, and Levi Woodbury.

"Czar Nicholas" Biddle, in a letter to Henry Clay, professed to be "delighted" with it.

It has all the fury of the unchained panther, biting the bars of his cage. It is really a manifesto of anarchy, such as Marat and Robespierre might have issued to the mob of the Faubourg St. Antoine; and my hope is that it will contribute to relieve the country from the domination of these miserable people.

He thought so highly of the veto message, indeed, that he had the Bank of the United States print thirty thousand copies of it for distribution, free, in the presidential election campaign of 1832. This the Bank, which was stigmatized in that very message as "a hydra of corruption," dutifully did. The cost was charged to its "stationery and printing" account, since Chestnut Street still insisted that it had no fund for political purposes. However, in that campaign alone it spent a total of $16,999—including $558 for the veto message—on similar giveaways, speeches by Clay, Webster, Ewing.

Andrew Jackson got 219 of the electoral votes. Henry Clay got 49. William Wirt got 7, all of them from Vermont.

The popular vote was: Jackson, 687,502; Clay *and* Wirt, 350,189.

William Morgan? They never did find him, dead or alive. The body hauled out of Oak Orchard Creek probably was that of Timothy Munroe, a farmhand who worked on the other side of Lake Ontario, in Canada, and who had been subject to fits of melancholia. At least, it was buried as Munroe.

Morgan's book, *Illustrations of Freemasonry, by One of the Fraternity who has Devoted Thirty Years to the Subject,* was published anyway, soon after his disappearance. The heavens did not fall.

18

THEY LOVED HIM
IN BEAN TOWN

Philip Hone, refined, retired, high-toned ex-mayor of New York, admired Andrew Jackson. Like so many other Easterners, he had gone to his first meeting with the President in a lather of trepidation, for he expected to be greeted by some yip-yawing critter with bowie knives at his belt, fire in his eye, and malapropisms tumbling out of his mouth. His disillusionment delighted him, and thereafter, whenever he was in Washington, he paid a courtesy call at the White House, for although he deplored the President's battle against the Bank, he enjoyed the company of this quiet-spoken old man.

He paid such a visit the night of March 4, 1833, just after Jackson had been inaugurated for the second time, and he was shocked by the appearance of the President, who "looks exceedingly feeble."

"If it were delicate and respectful to bet on such a subject," Hone told his diary later that night, "I would bet large odds that he does not outlive the present term of his office."

Robert B. Randolph would not have agreed with this. Randolph was a young naval lieutenant who had just been cashiered, and who somehow got it into his head that the President was to blame for it. The President, in fact, never had heard of the man.

On May 6 of 1833, a bright day, Randall went aboard an excursion steamer tied up at Alexandria, on the Potomac, preparatory to a trip to Rip Raps, a government-owned island in Chesapeake Bay that the President believed to be good for his health. The President himself was aboard, bending over a mass of work in the captain's cabin, his only companion the captain himself. There was no Secret Service then.

Randolph, all unchallenged, knocked on the cabin door. "Come in," the President called. Always accessible, he rose, stooping, and started to extend his hand. Ex-lieutenant Randolph burst in like an avenging angel and thrust his own right hand into the President's face.

He said afterward that all he meant to do was tweak the presidential nose, but there wasn't time to determine that. Andrew Jackson, screaming in rage, reached for his cane, rose full-length—and bumped his head against the cabin ceiling. The captain, who was nearby, grabbed the intruder and hustled him out onto the deck and down the gangplank, where a crowd, hearing of the incident in hasty snatches, and getting it all wrong, roughed him up by pushing him back and forth and demanded to know whether they should kill him.

The stunned President, appealed to, said no. He announced explosively that he would like to meet the rascal face to face, with any weapons or with none, but he certainly wasn't going to let somebody else do the task for him. On the wharf Randolph, lucky to be alive, was allowed to slip back into the nowhere from whence he had emerged.

On January 30, 1835, there was a more serious attack right in the Capitol, and a naval officer again was involved, this time as defender. The President had attended a state funeral for a prominent representative, and he was about to step out on the portico when Richard Lawrence, an English house painter, emerged from the crowd, pointed a pistol at him, and pulled the trigger. The pistol misfired. Lawrence promptly drew a second one, loaded like the other, but it, too, misfired. Andrew Jackson, not impeded this time by a low ceiling, raised his walking stick, and charged, bellowing in rage. His naval aide, Lieutenant Gedney, was even faster. Gedney clipped the man in the jaw, knocking him down, and then fell upon him, an act that quite possibly saved the poor fool's life and certainly spared him a caning.

It was the first time anybody had tried to assassinate a President of the United States. Lawrence, who kept telling everybody that he was a member of the British royal family, was sent to a lunatic asylum.

Andrew Jackson always declared that both of these assaults were the work of thugs hired by the Bank of the United States.

At about this time the Hero, after carrying it around for thirty years, decided to get rid of the pistol ball Jesse Benton had fired into his upper left arm. Such balls, as used then in affairs of honor, weighed an ounce and a half. Dickinson's was still too near the heart to be disturbed, but Benton's of late had nearly worked its way to the surface. Therefore, one afternoon, without any to-do, in his study, in the presence of a few friends who happened to be there anyway, Andrew Jackson took off his coat, rolled up his left shirt-sleeve, and ordered his old friend the surgeon general of the U.S. Army to cut the damn thing out. He took no laudanum, no painkiller of any kind, and did not bite a bullet. He simply stood there, watching, and when the chunk of lead fell to the floor he picked it up and gave it to a friend for a souvenir. After that he rolled down his sleeve, put his coat back on, and returned to his desk and his work.

No, this man was not ready to die. Not yet.

With all the exuberance of a boy getting out of school, he started on a tour of New England.

Unsmiling, though with an occasional wave, he rode through cheering crowds from Fredericksburg, Virginia, to Baltimore, to

Philadelphia, Newark, Elizabethtown, then by barge to New York.

At one point a bridge collapsed just after he had ridden across it. Again, a piece of wadding from a cannon whistled within inches of his head, disturbing him not the slightest. In New York the horse he rode bolted when a nearby saluting squad fired too soon. Dozens of men rushed to rescue the President, but he had the beast under control before they could get there.

In New York he was put up at the new American Hotel, next door to Philip Hone's house at 235 Broadway.

"The President is certainly the most popular man we have ever known," the ex-mayor remarked in his diary that night.

Washington was not so much so. His acts were popular, because all descriptions of men were ready to acknowledge him the "Father of His Country." But he was superior to the homage of the populace, too dignified, too grave for their liking, and men could not approach him with familiarity. Here is a man who suits them exactly. He has a kind expression for each—the same to all, no doubt, but each thinks it intended for himself. His manners are certainly good, and he makes the most of them. He is a *gourmand* of adulation, and by the assistance of the populace had persuaded himself that no man ever lived in the country to whom the country was so much indebted. Talk of him as the second Washington! It won't do now; Washington was only the first Jackson.

The analogy, which others have commented upon, was many-faceted. Both men, as noted, were incomparable equestrians, the best we ever had. Both hated crowds. Neither would slap a back, or permit his own to be slapped, much less kiss a baby. Washington didn't even like to shake hands and did so only when he thought it was his duty. And each took a tour of New England because he thought that he should, showing himself.

THEY LOVED HIM IN BEAN TOWN

They were the most painted of our presidents. They were
not vain men; yet each, though he found it boring to sit for
a portrait, was resigned to the recognition of his own immortality
and conceived it to be part of his job to see that posterity was
told what he looked like. Artists clamored to get at them, and
Jackson, like Washington, did not think it fair to refuse.
Throughout all the years of his administration a well-thought-of
dauber, Ralph E. W. Earl, lived in the White House with him,
"doing" him every time he got a chance.

Andrew Jackson was not the first President of the United
States who lacked a college education. George Washington was.
Washington worried about this. As a soldier he had felt the
need of advice, and whenever he could he consulted "real"
generals from abroad, like DeKalb, Pulaski, Conway, DeCoudray,
Steuben. As a national executive he was even more acutely aware
of what he supposed to be his shortcomings. Surrounded by
men like Marshall, Madison, Monroe, Jefferson, Randolph, Burr,
Jay, all of them college graduates, most of them honor students,
he was, intellectually, diffident. For one thing, he supposed that
he could not express himself well, certainly not in an elegant
manner, on paper, and the field command, like the presidency,
entailed an enormous correspondence, so that he soon found
himself surrounded by bright young secretaries, all of whom,
like Alexander Hamilton, the brightest, had been to college.

Washington was wrong. He had nothing to be ashamed
of in his writing style, which was lucid, never muddy. He commanded a large vocabulary, and he used his words with care,
seemingly without effort, though in fact he found all writing
an agony.

The Hero of New Orleans did not feel that way. Where
he came from, a course at college was not considered a gentle-
manly requisite. He could add and subtract, multiply and divide,
as well as the next man, and if his spelling was erratic, his
grammar shaky, why, these were faults to be found among the

181

perfumed popinjays of the East as well, so what of it? He could always make his point. The touches of fanciness, the "literary" bits, could be added later by men who had indeed listened to lectures within ivy-covered walls.

Andrew Jackson's official papers as President are among the finest in the archives. In his military messages he sometimes resorted to the brazen tarantaras that convention called for; in his political papers, never. Nor did he succumb to the temptation to display a knowledge of the classics that seized so many half-baked statesmen when they took pen in hand. He didn't, that is, resort to the trite, inappropriate metaphors of mythology. You will find nowhere in his writings a reference to the sword of Damocles, an Achilles' heel, a need to clean the Augean stable, Pandora's box, a Procrustean bed, and that rock to which Prometheus was chained.

"His mode of speech is slow and quiet," Harriet Martineau wrote after she had met him at the White House, "and his phraseology sufficiently betokens that his time has not been passed among books."

Not many were as gentle as this. It was the custom even before he came to the capital as President-elect to sneer at Jackson's diction and mimic his explosions of wrath. The teehee boys concentrated, as their superior upbringing entitled them to do, on his English. They made him into a monster of mistakes, and they glorified this queer creation so assiduously that in time it came to be almost real to them. Andrew Jackson was to be the first of those characteristically American creations, a line that was to include Daniel Boone, John L. Sullivan, and, more recently, Sam Goldwyn. "Include me out," belongs in the same class with "Elevate them guns a little lower"—perverted folklore.

When Jackson was invited by Harvard to accept an honorary Doctor of Laws degree, at least one shocked alumnus, ex-President John Quincy Adams, declined an invitation to attend the ceremony because, as he confided to his diary, though "an affectionate child" of the college he felt he could not "witness her disgrace in conferring her highest literary honors upon a barbarian who could not write a sentence of grammar and could hardly spell his own name." Nevertheless, the affair was a great success, the President acting, as he always did, with impeccable dignity. When he was about to leave the platform, some wag is said to have called out, "All right, you're a doctor now! Let's hear some Latin!" The President turned with a grin, crying, "Certainly. *Pax vobiscum e pluribus unum.*" Although the story was widely believed, it was obviously untrue, for at least two reasons: (1) Andrew Jackson could not grin; and (2) he didn't know that many Latin words.

His syntax, such as it was, was sound enough. Occasionally in the letters—and it must be assumed in his informal speech—such a usage as "have drank" crops up, but the meaning is always plain. The spelling is something else.

English spelling at that time had not been standardized, if indeed it can be said to be standardized even now. John C. Calhoun himself, who got straight A's at Yale, habitually misspelled that shipwreck rock of so many spelling bees, *separation*, which he wrote with two *e*'s and one *a*. Many of the words in Jackson's letters, which have caused exquisitely educated readers to snigger—words like *cloathing, vissit, publick, watchfull, warr*—were common usages in his time, holdovers from the eighteenth century, though *quiett, valluable, parsomony, betalions,* and, above all, *amonghest,* seem to have been distinctly his own. He did repeatedly write *secrete* for *secret, councel* for *council,* and *goverement* and *degredation.*

The most extraordinary charge brought against him was that he invented *O.K.*

You hear it in Rangoon, Cairo, Shanghai, everywhere. Moonfaced shopkeepers beam at you and say "O.K." Spirited sprigs of the benighted heathen in unpronounceable parts of the world cry "O.K." as they smirk. Few of them would pretend to know another word of English, but they do know this one.

Where did it come from? It oozed into the public prints without fanfare at just about the time that Andrew Jackson started to move his effects into 1600 Pennsylvania Avenue, but there is not a scintilla of evidence to suggest that he had anything to do with its birth. The knowledgeable, determined to have their quaint character, have asserted that President Jackson, when new on the job, instead of signing papers used to mark them "Oll Korrect," which the old fool later shortened to "O.K."

This is preposterous. The boll weevils of research have burrowed among his presidential papers and even all the papers that had passed across his desk when he was chief justice of the Tennessee supreme court, but have found no such usage, although the words *all* and *correct*, spelled correctly, often occur in the letters.

There have been many suggested explanations of *O.K.,* most of them mere guesses.

Old-time schoolmasters in England used to mark papers *Omnis Korrecta,* in Greek, but there is no evidence that this was ever practiced in America.

Rum that came from Aux Cayes, Haiti, at that time was considered the best, infallibly good, and of course Aux Cayes was pronounced (and still is), "O.K."

There was a freight dispatcher in Cincinnati whose name was O'Kelly, or possibly it was Obadiah Kelly, and who chalked the initials O.K. on boxcars that had been checked and were ready to go. This story would stand up better if there were not so many extant examples of *O.K.* being used in newspapers both east and west, in exactly its present sense, long before Cincinnati *had* a railroad.

Okeh, spelled that way, is a Choctaw word meaning "It is so." The Choctaws were one of the more "civilized" tribes of the Creek confederacy, and almost anybody who dealt with them, including Andrew Jackson, would be familiar with the word.

Yet the only person who appears to have subscribed to this theory is the late Woodrow Wilson, who used to mark White House memos "okeh."

Shipbuilding people at one time pointed out that when clippers were abuilding in American yards it was customary to mark the planks, prepared at a separate shop, according to where they would go when the vessel was assembled. The most important of these, the call for which meant that construction was really under way, were marked "O.K.," which stood for "outer keel." Not even many shipbuilding people ever believed this. For one thing, O.K. appeared in the West, in places many miles from deep water.

There was a highly thought-of Indian chief called Keokuk (Keokuk, Iowa, was named after him) who was always referred to as Old Keokuk, after which the speaker almost invariably added "He's all right!" This, however, does not explain the early appearance in print of O.K. in such places as Portsmouth and Boston. Keokuk was a Sauk.

Lexicographers, like economists, always disagree with one another. Doubtless the discussion about the origin of America's best-known phrase will go on and on, as long as the learned can perceive new reasons why those seemingly unrelated letters, O and K, should, when juxtaposed, signify assent. No matter. It is worthy of remark, though, that the latest theory, one seemingly accepted by so careful a critic as H. L. Mencken, who based his approval on an *American Speech* article by the late Allen Walker Reid (July 19, 1941), passes the honor on to Jackson's small yes-man, Martin Van Buren:

That evidence was to the effect that O.K. made its first appearance in print in the New York *New Era* on March 23, 1840, that it was then part of the name of the Democratic O.K. Club, an organization of supporters of Martin Van Buren for a second term in the White House, and that it was an abbreviation of Old Kinderhook, the name of the Hudson Valley village in which he had been born in 1782.

The association of Kinderhook with his name was by no means new. He had been known to his enemies since the early days of the Albany Regency as the *Kinderhook Fox,* and to his followers as the *Sage, Magician* or *Wizard* of *Kinderhook,* and it was thus natural for one of the rowdy clubs which supported him in New York to call itself after the little town. Who thought of reducing the name to O.K. is not known but it was in accord with the liking for secrecy and mystification that marked the politics of the time. The Democratic O.K. Club held its first recorded meeting in the house of Jacob Colvin, at 245 Grand street, on March 24, 1840, and the new name caught on at once. It was brief, it had a masculine and even bellicose ring, and it was mysterious enough to have a suggestion of the sinister.

Andrew Jackson did not adopt the practice of his predecessor and "spread" the prestige of a visit by staying at a different inn each night, so that the delighted owners could advertise (as their heirs still do) "George Washington Slept Here," but he did visit a good many towns. There were Providence and Newport, and after Boston there were Cambridge, Salem, Concord, and Lowell. Here his physicians called a halt, and turned him around, and hurried him back to Washington nonstop, being afraid that they would not get him there in time.

But he was durable, this Hero. He never stopped snarling.

19

THE CASE OF THE FRENCH IMBROGLIO

The Bank of the United States was not dead. As the wags put it, it had been "Biddled, diddled, and undone." It did not stir, did not even twitch, but the President believed that there was life in it yet, and that it was only biding its time, playing 'possum.

The election of 1832 was contested on a single issue. On one side had been Old Hickory and Martin Van Buren; on the other, Henry Clay, the Bank's principal apologist, and, as vice-presidential candidate, John Sergeant of Philadelphia, one of the Bank's salaried lawyers and a close personal friend of Nicholas Biddle. The administration had won, and that should have been enough. Both sides should have assumed that the war was over and turned their attention to something else. Neither did.

Back from New England, President Jackson, with the Blairs for company, went to Rip Raps for a month of thought and sea air. Even then he was considering an order to cease deposits of federal funds in the Bank of the United States. Understand: he did not plan to take out deposits *already there*, only to refrain from making new ones. The result would be the same—the drying-up of BUS resources, the sapping of BUS strength—but the distinction was more than just fancy phraseology.

The President could not see why the government should keep on feeding money into a private corporation that had been, as he saw it, disowned by the public. The Bank, of course, was unconstitutional in the first place, the President believed, though he admitted that this never could be established in law as long as John Marshall clung to his life.

Nicholas Biddle, urbane, cheerful, was nevertheless preparing for a fund-removal move. He was calling in loans, putting pressure on state banks, paving the way for an inflation scare, which could of course be blamed on the administration. He was tightening his grip upon the press, at least eighty percent of which was already under his control. Editors in those days were usually the owners of their papers, and most operated on something less than a shoestring. They were dependent upon their local banks because so many of their advertisers were, which meant that they were dependent upon Nicholas Biddle, who was now for the first time flexing his fiscal muscles.

"Czar Nicholas" deprived the five government members of the Bank's board of their various committee chairmanships, a show of strength that was childish and not worthy of the man. He was in complete command of the board, without the need to harrass government members, who were never more than decoration.

The Hero came back from Rip Raps with blood in his eye. So Mr. Biddle wanted to fight? Good! He ordered the Secretary of the Treasury to cease depositing public moneys in the Bank of the United States. The Secretary refused. The President fired him.

Andrew Jackson was not an executive who was hard on his aides. He was no "backwoods Caesar," as the National Republicans liked to call him. True, he had had four Secretaries of State, five of the Treasury, three of War, three Navy, three Attorneys General, and two Postmasters General, and that was esteemed by the head-waggers, the tongue-cluckers, as bad, irresponsible, in fact. For the most part, however, the changes had been made quietly and without rancor, with a good reason behind each one.

Even in the case of William J. Duane, the Hero displayed no haste, no vindictiveness. Duane was a Pennsylvania politico, and he had not previously been notable for independence of thought. He had not been in the cabinet long, and he was known to be a believer in the Bank. That could also be said of others closer to the President—Major Lewis, Louis McLane, Edward Livingston—but the Hero did not hold it against them. However, the treasury was different. The law that had created this department provided that only the secretary could take such an action as Andrew Jackson was proposing. The President couldn't do it alone, *as* President. He argued quietly with William J. Duane for five days, and then he called for the man's resignation and appointed in his place Roger Taney, who promptly ordered that all deposits be withheld from the Bank.

Biddle was prepared for this. As soon as what the press persisted in calling the withdrawal order was issued, petitions began to pour in on Congress and the President. They came from clubs and societies, fraternities, boards of trade, chambers of commerce, even (in New England) some church congregations. They pointed to the skyrocketing of prices, and pleaded for relief. One and all, they had the same cry: the Bank must be continued.

It was clear to the President that the forces of evil were intent upon bringing about financial chaos, a condition that could then be used as proof that the nation needed the Bank. It was the weakness of Jackson's position that he had no substitute or successor ready, he proposed no alternative. His genius was destructive. He was good at tearing down, not so good at building up. He could cry that what Biddle was setting out to do proved what he himself had charged: that the Bank, under its one-man control, could in a fit of vengeance ruin the credit of the whole country. But he had no cure to offer. He had, it would seem, not even given thought to what his Vice President, Van Buren, was rather timorously proposing: the making of the Bank of the United States into an integral department of the government (the subtreasury system that was eventually to be adopted).

Jackson instead ordered that the federal funds be deposited in state banks here and there. These institutions were immediately called the "pet banks," and the charge was made that corruption had entered into the selection of them. This charge was false and easily refuted, but the damage had been done, and the American public, then as now, was notoriously reluctant to listen to denials.

Meanwhile, Henry Clay was trying another tack.

One of the very last acts of the House before Congress adjourned in 1833 had been the adoption, by a narrow vote, of a resolution "that Government deposits may . . . be safely continued in the Bank of the United States." This resolution was duly handed to President Jackson on the last day of his first term, and duly acknowledged, then forgotten. In the new Congress, however, Clay must have had it in mind when he introduced on December 26 a couple of resolutions that have no counterpart in American history.

The first of these resolved "That the President in the late executive proceedings in relation to the public revenue, has assumed upon himself authority and power not conferred by the Constitution and the laws, but in derogation of both."

The second resolved "That the reasons assigned by the Secretary (of the Treasury) for the removal are unsatisfactory and insufficient."

Here was an act without precedent, a vote of censure of the President of the United States by the Senate of the United States, not to mention the Secretary of the Treasury. What Clay hoped to accomplish by it we cannot know. He must have been aware that it had no standing. His own explanation, a lame one, was that under the law establishing the Department of the Treasury the secretary became an agent of Congress rather than an agent of the President, and perhaps because of the last-minute resolution of the previous House (Mr. Clay was especially vague on this point) the secretary could be thought to have been directed by Congress to continue to deposit federal funds in the Bank of the United States. When Roger Taney then obeyed the order of the President rather than that of the now defunct House of Representatives of the Congress of 1831, he was committing an illegal act.

Had the Taney censure resolution stood alone, there might have been found a smidgen of sense to this argument. But in view of the resolution censuring the President himself, it was preposterous. The President, after all, was authorized by the Constitution to appoint a Secretary of the Treasury, and so he was authorized to remove that same secretary.

One possible explanation of Clay's move was that he sought to discredit the President with a view to forestalling a third-term attempt. People already were beginning to talk about a third term.

The President himself promptly replied to the censure resolution with a detailed defense of his position, but the Senate refused to accept it and sent it back without having spread it on the record.

The censure resolutions themselves were admirably brief. Clay's presentation of them was not. He took three full days over it. The three following days were taken by Thomas Hart Benton, who declared that everything Senator Clay had just said was wrong.

The President had other things to think about. There were, for instance, foreign affairs.

In the field of foreign affairs many of his followers feared for Andrew Jackson. They might admire him as a soldier, a planter, even as a domestic arbiter, but as a statesman he was, to them, inconceivable. When he was among friends or even among familiar enemies, fellow countrymen, his fiery temper could be countered. But what about diplomats?

191

ANDREW JACKSON, HERO

There is a classic definition: when a diplomat says yes he means perhaps; when he says perhaps he means no; when he says no he is no diplomat. Jackson had been a no-sayer from 'way back. Moreover, his refusals were not simply enunciated, they were shouted.

In all matters domestic the Hero was proving to be just what the country had needed, but his friends trembled and turned pale when they thought of what might happen when he was faced with a problem of international significance.

Yet in the first crisis it was the President, in person, unprompted, who uttered the soft answer that turned away wrath.

The Texans had won their independence and clamored to be recognized as a preliminary to annexation. The Mexicans, of course, objected. That the Hero's heart was with the Texans all his friends knew, and later, when he had come to believe that Great Britain might be interested in taking over that vast empty territory, presumably because it offered a path to New Orleans and control of the Mississippi, Andrew Jackson was outspoken in his approval of annexation. When the Texas delegation came to him, early in his first term, however, he made the only answer that would have averted war. He reminded them, gently, that the United States had a nonaggression pact with the Republic of Mexico. And that was that.

Jackson had inherited the West Indian trade dispute. Ever since the Revolution, and especially since the War of 1812, Great Britain had prohibited American trade with its West Indian possessions. It was mostly a matter of food. The planters there in fact were *not* there; they were absentee owners, running their profitable places through agents and overseers on the spot. Meanwhile, they themselves gloried in the salubrious climate of home and bought themselves titles and parliamentary seats in order to protect their faraway interests. The Sugar Aristocracy, they were called. These persons would gladly have done business with Yankee traders, who were in a position to supply their island needs—breadstuffs, salted fish, horses for meat—as the English traders, even with the assistance of the Royal Navy, were not. The latter for a long time prevailed, and tried in vain to divert this trade to eastern Canada. The result was that smuggling, always bad in those parts, was growing worse all the time, and the system was wasteful.

John Quincy Adams, himself a New Englander, and considered the country's leading expert on foreign affairs, had wrestled with this problem for eight years, four as Secretary of State under Monroe, four as President, and he had come up with nothing.

The Hero assigned Martin Van Buren to the task as soon as he appointed him to the first cabinet, and Van Buren did it. It took time, and tact. The English ministers, squeezed between the Sugar Aristocracy on one side and the "legitimate" local traders on the other, for a long while held out for the status quo—that is, the restrictions, virtually a ban, on American trade in the West Indies—but Marty Van liked Englishmen, who liked him, and he was a master of the art of face-saving. At last, therefore, he came up with a solution that almost everybody could approve.

The French Imbroglio was a much more prickly object, a veritable porcupine to pick up.

Napoleon Bonaparte has been hailed as a military genius, which is odd when we consider that he lost more battles than he won, including the most important one, the last. He was also ruinously spendthrift. Napoleon's formula for victory was the old-fashioned one of getting there first with the most men, and unlike Julius Caesar, Gustavus Adolphus, the Duke of Marlborough, and Frederick the Great, he contributed to the art of land fighting no turning-point novelty such as the second line, the holding movement, the counter-counterattack, the horse artillery.

He may have been a *political* genius. He thought he was,

anyway. In the course of his traipsing back and forth across Europe with his various armies he was to promulgate through a series of decrees—the Berlin decree of November 21, 1806; the Milan of November 11, 1807; Bayonne, April 5, 1808; Vienna (a secret decree) in August of 1809; and Rambouillet, March 23, 1810—what he was pleased to call his Continental System. These decrees played hob with established economics, not to mention the rules of modern warfare. They caused the confiscation of vast properties, often in the form of shipping, from the conquered nations as well as some that had been neutral, such as the United States. Bonaparte had planned his system well, and it just might have worked, if he'd won. But he didn't win. He lost.

In 1815 the other nations of Europe descended unpent upon a beaten France in search of repayment. Great chunks of what was left of the Continental System were doled out among the victors, but the United States got none of them, for it was not present at the dismemberment. The American claims were valid, however, and in due time this country began to make diplomatic arrangements with certain peripheral governments for the collection of spoliations claims. Russia, Denmark, Portugal, the Netherlands, and the two Sicilies, all had been compliant, and recently John Nelson, Jackson's minister to Naples, had accepted $2,119,230 in full payment from that former Napoleonic captive. France, however, remained aloof. French spoliations claims from 1803 to 1815 totaled over $12,000,000 without interest. The exact amount was yet to be determined, as was the amount, certainly much smaller, that the United States owed France for the same reasons. The whole business was incredibly complicated.

France had been obliged to accept a king thrust upon it by the victors, first Louis XVIII, then Charles X, both of them Bourbons, and its political leaders were desperately trying to hold down taxes lest they find themselves with another revolution on their hands. Charles X was no help. The real rulers in Paris then were the principal ambassadors, the British, Prussian, Russian, and Austrian.

America? It could wait.

Andrew Jackson thought not. America already had waited too long. Its claim was clear, its cause just, and it should not be shoved aside. He sent William Cabell Rives, a Virginian, to Paris as ambassador, his orders being to collect those long-deferred debts.

Rives did wonders, but it was uphill work, a long climb. The first foreign minister he encountered, the Prince de Polignac, refused to agree that France was financially responsible for the acts of Bonaparte, although treaties with virtually every other nation in the Western world acknowledged this responsibility. Off the record, Polignac pointed out that it would be as much as his political neck was worth to admit the obligation. He continued to prevaricate.

Rives pressed on, doggedly, relentlessly. The ambassador was not permitted to confront the Chamber of Deputies in person, as he would have liked, but must treat through the foreign office. When some deputy found the word *force* in one of President Jackson's messages to Congress and insisted that this was a "threat" to France, Rives was able to contend that there had been a poor translation and that *force*, used in this sense, did not mean what the deputy seemed to think it meant, adding quietly that a presidential message was an internal government paper anyway, with which the French had nothing to do. When somebody else came up with the embarrassing fact that there was a clause in the Louisiana Purchase treaty of 1803 that virtually assured France of most-favored-nation treatment at the port of New Orleans, Rives was able to smooth that over as well, in part by promising to have the United States tariff on French wines cut.

At last, and just as it was beginning to look as though the French had been cornered, there was another flipflop on high.

Charles X was forced to leave the country, and his cousin, Louis-Philippe, of the house of Orleans, was proclaimed "King of the French by the grace of God and the will of the people." Rives had to start all over again.

Louis-Philippe was an amiable nincompoop who tried to be as unaristocratic as possible, and he liked Americans, saw the justice of their demands, and would have helped them had he possessed any power. By this time Edward Livingston, who had lately succeeded Martin Van Buren as Secretary of State, was recommending to the President that "energetic measures" be used in order to get France to pay the debt. Rives, however, quietly persisted, and at last he got a treaty, signed in Paris on July 4, 1831.

The United States immediately cut the tariff on wines and made out an order for 1,500,000 francs to be paid to France in settlement of its claims against this country. But when the Secretary of the Treasury turned over to the Bank of the United States for collection a bill for 25,000,000 francs, as agreed in Paris, all he got back was a second-hand snub, together with a BUS bill of $175,000 for services in trying to collect, plus protest fees, etc., all perfectly legal. The Bank's bill was paid. The King was sorry, the ministers were sorry, but only the deputies could authorize the appropriation of such a sum for such a purpose, and the deputies were still playing hard to get.

Rives had returned to Virginia, and Livingston himself was appointed ambassador to France, a post he had asked for.

President Jackson was waxing sore. He snarled. He ordered the U.S. Navy to put itself into a state of readiness. In his annual message of 1834 he asked Congress to take reprisals on French property in the United States. The House agreed; the Senate said no. The Chamber of Deputies screamed that France had been insulted.

The French ambassador to the United States asked for his passports. The American ambassador to France did the same, although first he reminded the French ministers again that presidential messages to Congress were internal matters with which France should have nothing to do. When this plea was ignored he retired only as far as Holland, leaving the embassy in charge of a *chargé d'affaires.*

Here was a real war scare.

Lord Palmerston, the British foreign minister, offered his services as mediator. Palmerston was eager to keep the friendship of France in order to maintain pressure against Russia, which was again trying to snatch some land from Turkey. Therefore, it may be assumed that his judgment would have gone against the United States, if his offer had been accepted, which it was not. Things happened fast now, and with a swinging goodwill. Livingston, freshly instructed, returned to Paris with a new offer, an offer that included something the deputies were able to construe as an apology, although President Jackson certainly had not meant it to be that. The money was paid. The French Imbroglio was at an end.

And so, almost, was the presidency of General Jackson.

20

HAIL TO THE
BIG PIECE OF CHEESE!

That the American public, or at least a large and very noisy part of it, had taken Andrew Jackson to its heart was evident at that first "welcoming day" at the White House. It was just as evident at the multitude's last day and night there.

His admirers liked to give him gifts. Other Presidents had been given things, but these were usually of a formal nature, whereas Jackson's were homey things, personal things, handed him with an air of spontaneity. Many of them were made of hickory: walking sticks, of course, canes, scores of them. But there were also chairs, tables, hat racks, flagpoles, even a light carriage, a phaeton, all made of hickory, memorializing his nickname. He did not utilize the phaeton, nor did he ever ride in the larger vehicle made out of planks torn from the U.S.S. *Constitution* and given him by admiring New Englanders as a memento of his visit to their part of the country. When he rode forth he preferred to be astraddle a horse, the more spirited the better, although when the occasion called for it he used the Executive Mansion's own coach, driven, of course, by Charles, the huge proud black who was the Hero's own property, and who even now was packing to go back to Tennessee with the General.

The quaint custom in those times was to celebrate Washington's Birthday on February 22, which is the anniversary of the birth of the Father of His Country, and it was February 22, 1837, when Andrew Jackson gave his last big bash at the Executive Mansion. The party was a sort of open house, as the first had been, and was attended by just about everybody. It was a glorious splash of Southern hospitality. Food was served, and liquor and wines, there was music, and sometimes, briefly, the President himself, who, very ill, would venture from his closestool now and then to come halfway downstairs. There, in dressing robe and bedroom slippers, he would apologetically greet as many of his guests as could get to him.

But the biggest attraction of all was a cheese, four feet across and weighing fourteen hundred pounds. It was a farewell gift from one T. S. Meachum, an Oswego County, New York, dairy farmer, not otherwise known to fame. It was the biggest cheese in the world.

Sitting up there in his study—though from time to time he might make it to the couch, to lie down for a little while—Jackson must have wondered what they would do with that cheese. He certainly couldn't take it back to Tennessee with him. Besides, shouldn't it be considered as national property now, like the furniture in the Executive Mansion?

The sounds from below reached him as a sort of muffled clatter, punctuated by the unremitting click-thunk of the big front door as folks came and went. How many of them were there? This was going to cost him a pretty penny, just when he would be needing money to go home. The job here brought him $25,000 a year, in monthly payments, but there was no allowance for expenses, and entertaining could ruin any President.

It would be good to get back to the Hermitage. Jackson sighed. This White House, as they were calling it, was a comfortable enough place, and convenient, once you got used to it, but it was not home and never would be. He tended to rattle around here. There were even times when he felt like thanking the Eternal for those damned rapscallions up on the Hill, who at least kept him busy.

He was sixty-six, nearly sixty-seven, and feeling every bit of it. He could hear his valet moving tentatively about the room—a black servant, one of his own, brought from Tennessee, not a part of the regular household staff here—and he summoned him with a cough. He had meant to lie down for a little while, but when he got to his feet he felt a mite stronger, better able to control his gut, so he decided to take advantage of this lull in the pain and go downstairs for a time.

They half carried him there, and he clung to a banister as he nodded recognition, remembering names. The din was deafening. He knew that he could not stay long, for it made him dizzy.

He noticed that they had solved the problem of what to do with the cheese. They were cutting it into small wedges and wrapping them in paper and handing them out as souvenirs to the departing guests, just as is done with the cake at an elegant wedding reception.

That was good, a good plan. But they'd better start making those pieces larger and larger. It was getting late, and fourteen hundred pounds of cheese is a lot of cheese.

He felt a borborygmus rumble from his innards, which he hoped none of those who had climbed up here to the fifth step had heard, and he knew that he had better get back upstairs. He whispered to the servant, murmured apologies to those who were seeking to shake his hand, and permitted himself to be led off.

Seated again, he reflected upon the worries that he'd met in this mansion. He had struggled past them as best he knew how, and he only hoped that nobody had noticed any hesitancy on his part. There was pretty Peg Eaton and all that cabinet stir. There was his Rotation of Office plan, which had not been popular, though he believed that it had done much good when he shook up the Establishment. He had pointed the way toward getting the redskins to cross the Mississippi to lands where they would surely be happier—and safer. The Texans he had taken care of, and the evasive Frenchies, and those New England shipping interests that had been so concerned about the sugar islands commerce.

Of course he had vetoed their precious Maysville Road bill, and he knew that this had brought him many enemies, but he could point with joy to the fact that the national debt had been done away with right at the time he'd said it would—the end of 1834.

He hiccupped thoughtfully, then winced in pain. Even that slight motion of his innards hurt. The servant came over, but the Hero shook his head.

And—the Bank! Now there was his greatest triumph! He had slain the Monster of Chestnut Street, decreeing as he did so that the United States should take care of its own money instead of entrusting it to the care of private bankers. Posterity would see this deed in its proper light, and would thank him for it, no matter how the Eastern millionaires might growl.

He had frowned down those damned nullificationists, and he was proud of that, yes. He had spiked John Calhoun's high-falutin plans for a Southern conspiracy to which Washington would have to defer for permission every time it wanted to do something for the people. He had appointed Roger Taney to the Supreme Court after John Marshall at long last had consented to die, and that made three right-thinking men there now.

Yes, he had managed to do many things that badly needed doing. But the greatest achievement of them all was the skewering of the United States Bank.

He chuckled, and there was very little pain. The laudanum was catching hold. Soon he might be able to get some sleep.

The noise downstairs had dimmed, and the click-thunk of the door sounded less often.

Mr. Clay and his National Republicans—they were beginning to call themselves Whigs—had tried very hard, with his pestiferous "censure," to take the edge off that victory. Well, he'd failed. Tom Benton, tough old Tom, had seen to that. He had fought Mr. Clay's resolution tooth and nail, the only way he knew, and when it had passed despite his protests he had warned the Senate that he would not rest until he had seen that misjustice undone. He wanted the thing stricken from the record, he had said. He wanted it expunged.

He had prevailed, though it took him the better part of three years, during which time the United States Senate had little chance to conduct any business that was not routine. The fight had ended only the other day, with the damned "Whigs" in full retreat.

Much of the last part of the battle was concerned with semantics. The President's friends in effect had gone to the people, who rallied to the Hero, fairly inundating their senators with letters and resolutions of disapproval. Benton had insisted that the offensive resolution be "expunged" from the record. *Expunge,* this learned roughneck told his fellow solons, meant strike out, blot out, erase. It meant, literally, originally, to "prick out," from the Latin *ex,* out, and *pungere,* to prick. He would settle for nothing less. The Whigs, in consternation, or perhaps just stalling for more time, had cried that they could not do this; it would be illegal. The Constitution empowered the Senate to keep a record of its proceedings, but it said nothing about alteration or erasure.

Benton held to his point, and at last the Whigs capitulated. On January 16, 1837, Senator Benton offered a florid resolution that authorized the clerk of the Senate to draw black lines around that particular entry in the official journal, and to write across it "Expunged by Order of the Senate." This the clerk did, right there in front of all of them.

Remembering, the man on the close-stool chuckled, and when this was followed by no pain he guessed he could maybe get some sleep now. He called the servant, who worked him to bed.

A few days later the outgoing President escorted the incoming President, Martin Van Buren, to the Capitol for the inauguration. There had been some resentment, rumor said, at the fact that the Hero had issued a Farewell Message, which could be regarded as a rebuke to the Father of His Country, though many preferred to find it a compliment. *He* didn't care, of course. He had done what he thought was right.

No such resentment showed in the crowd, which obviously had come to cheer the one who was going out rather than the dapper little man who was coming in. Old Hickory was about to be replaced by Slippery Elm, men muttered. Business was bad, and getting worse. Inflation loomed. But the day was lovely.

A few days after that the ex-President left Washington. The Hermitage had burned during his absence and had been rebuilt under his orders at long distance. Young Jack, his son, had not made a good thing of the plantation. There were claims amounting to at least $10,000 against it. The Hero of New Orleans had had about $5,000 in his pocket when he went to Washington eight years ago. He had $90 when he left. And he was not entitled to a pension.

He was the first President to leave by railroad. He took the B&O as far as Ellicott's Mills, Maryland, the western terminus of the line. Then he went by stagecoach to Wheeling, and then by steamer to Nashville, which was an easy horseback jog from the Hermitage. The trip took eighteen days, and he was very tired when at last he got home. He went right to bed.

BIBLIOGRAPHY

Abernethy, Thomas Perkins. *From Frontier to Plantation in Tennessee: A Study in Frontier Democracy.* Chapel Hill: University of North Carolina Press, 1932.

Adams, Charles Francis. *See* Adams, John Quincy.

Adams, Henry. *John Randolph.* Boston: Houghton Mifflin Company, 1898.

Adams, John Quincy. *Memoirs of John Quincy Adams.* Charles Francis Adams, ed. 12 vols. Philadelphia: J. B. Lippincott & Co., 1874-77.

Alexander, Holmes. *The American Talleyrand: The Career and Contemporaries of Martin Van Buren, Eighth President.* New York: Russell & Russell, 1968.

Bancroft, Frederic. *Calhoun and the South Carolina Nullification Movement.* Baltimore: The Johns Hopkins Press, 1928.

———. *The Life of William H. Seward.* 2 vols. New York: Harper and Brothers Publishers, 1900.

Bassett, John Spencer. *The Life of Andrew Jackson.* New York: The Macmillan Company, 1928.

———. "Major Lewis on the Nomination of Andrew Jackson." *Proceedings of the American Antiquarian Society,* New Series, Vol. 33 (Worcester, Mass., 1924), pp. 12-33.

———. *See* Jackson, Andrew.

Bemis, Samuel Flagg. *A Diplomatic History of the United States.* New York: Henry Holt and Company, 1936.

Benton, Thomas Hart. *Thirty Years View: or, A History of the Working of the American Government for Thirty Years, from 1820 to 1850.* 2 vols. New York: D. Appleton Company, 1854.

Beveridge, Albert J. *The Life of John Marshall.* 4 vols. Boston: Houghton Mifflin Company, 1929.

Bobbe, Dorothie. *DeWitt Clinton.* New York: Milton, Balch & Company, 1933.

Boucher, Chauncey Samuel. *The Nullification Controversy in South Carolina.* Chicago: University of Chicago Press, 1916.

Bowers, Claude G. *The Party Battles of the Jackson Period.* Boston: Houghton Mifflin Company, 1922.

BIBLIOGRAPHY

Bradford, Gamaliel. *As God Made Them*. Boston: Houghton Mifflin Company, 1929.

Buell, Augustus C. *History of Andrew Jackson: Pioneer, Soldier, Politician, President*. 2 vols. New York: Charles Scribner's Sons, 1904.

Byrdsall, F. *The History of the Loco-Foco or Equal Rights Party: Its Movements, Conventions and Proceedings*. New York: Clement & Packard, 1842.

Capers, Gerald M. *John C. Calhoun, Opportunist: A Reappraisal*. Gainesville: University of Florida Press, 1960.

Cash, W. J. *The Mind of the South*. New York: Alfred A. Knopf, 1958.

Catterall, Ralph C. H. *The Second Bank of the United States*. Chicago: Chicago University Press, 1903.

Cave, Alfred A. *Jacksonian Democracy and the Historians*. Gainesville: University of Florida Press, 1964.

Chitwood, Oliver Perry. *John Tyler, Champion of the Old South*. New York: D. Appleton-Century Company, 1939.

Coit, Margaret L. *John C. Calhoun: American Portrait*. Boston: Houghton Mifflin Company, 1950.

Current, Richard N. *Daniel Webster and the Rise of National Conservatism*. Boston: Little, Brown and Company, 1955.

Curtis, James C. *The Fox at Bay: Martin Van Buren and the Presidency, 1837-1841*. Lexington, Ky.: The University of Kentucky Press, 1970.

Debo, Angie. *A History of the Indians of the United States*. Norman, Okla.: University of Oklahoma Press, 1970.

————. *The Road to Disappearance*. Norman, Okla: University of Oklahoma Press, 1941.

Eaton, Clement. *Henry Clay and the Art of American Politics*. Boston: Little, Brown and Company, 1957.

————, ed. *The Leaven of Democracy: The Growth of the Democratic Spirit in the Time of Jackson*. New York: George Braziller, 1963.

Fish, Carl Russell. *The Civil Service and the Patronage*. Cambridge, Mass.: Harvard University Press, 1920.

Fitzpatrick, John C. *See* Van Buren, Martin.

Foreman, Grant. *Indian Removal: The Emigration of the Five Civilized Tribes of Indians*. Norman, Okla.: University of Oklahoma Press, 1956.

Fox, Dixon Ryan. *The Decline of Aristocracy in the Politics of New York.* New York: Columbia University Press, 1919.

Fraser, Hugh Russell. *Democracy in the Making: The Jackson-Tyler Era.* Indianapolis: The Bobbs-Merrill Company, 1938.

Freehling, William W., ed. *The Nullification Era: A Documentary Record.* New York: Harper and Row, 1967.

Gammon, Samuel Rhea. *The Presidential Campaign of 1832.* Baltimore: The Johns Hopkins Press, 1922.

Gatell, Frank Otto, and McFaul, John M. "The Outcast Insider: Reuben M. Whitney and the Bank War." *The Pennsylvania Magazine of History and Biography,* Vol. XCI, No. 2 (April 1967), pp. 115-44.

——, eds. *Jacksonian America, 1815-1840: New Society, Changing Politics.* Englewood Cliffs, N.J.: Prentice-Hall, 1970.

Gordon, T. F. *The War on the Bank of the United States, 1834.* New York: Augustus M. Kelley, Publishers, 1968.

Gosnell, Harold Foote. *See* Merriam, Charles Edward.

Govan, Thomas Payne. *Nicholas Biddle: Nationalist and Public Banker, 1786-1844.* Chicago: University of Chicago Press, 1959.

Gunderson, Robert Gray. *The Log-Cabin Campaign.* Lexington, Ky.: University of Kentucky Press, 1957.

Hacker, Louis M. *The Triumph of American Capitalism: The Development of Forces in American History to the End of the Nineteenth Century.* New York: Simon & Schuster, 1940.

Hammond, Bray. *Banks and Politics in America, from the Revolution to the Civil War.* Princeton, N.J.: Princeton University Press, 1957.

Hammond, Jared Delano. *The History of Political Parties in the State of New York.* New York: H. & E. Phinney, 1846.

Herring, Pendleton. *The Politics of Democracy: American Parties in Action.* New York: W. W. Norton & Company, 1940.

Hoffman, William S. *Andrew Jackson and North Carolina Politics.* Chapel Hill, N.C.: University of North Carolina Press, 1958.

Hofstadter, Richard. *The American Political Tradition and the Men Who Made It.* New York: Vintage Books, 1954.

——. *The Idea of a Party System: The Rise of Legitimate Opposition in the United States, 1780-1840.* Berkeley and Los Angeles: University of California Press, 1969.

BIBLIOGRAPHY

Hone, Philip. *The Diary of Philip Hone, 1828-1851.* Allan Nevins, ed. 2 vols. New York: Dodd, Mead and Company, 1927.

Houston, David Franklin. *A Critical Study of Nullification in South Carolina.* New York: Longmans, Green, and Co., 1896.

Hudson, Frederic. *Journalism in the United States, from 1690 to 1872.* New York: Harper & Brothers, 1873.

Hugins, Walter. *Jacksonian Democracy and the Working Class.* Stanford, Calif.: Stanford University Press, 1960.

Jackson, Andrew. *The Correspondence of Andrew Jackson,* John Spencer Bassett, ed. 6 vols. Washington: The Carnegie Institution of Washington, 1926-35.

James, Marquis. *Andrew Jackson, The Border Captain.* Indianapolis: The Bobbs-Merrill Company, 1933.

——. *Andrew Jackson: Portrait of a President.* Indianapolis: The Bobbs-Merrill Company, 1940.

Jones, W. Melville, ed. *Chief Justice John Marshall: A Reappraisal.* Ithaca, N.Y.: Cornell University Press, 1956.

Kauffman, Henry J. *The Pennsylvania Kentucky Rifle.* New York: Bonanza Books, 1960.

Longaker, Richard P. "Was Jackson's Kitchen Cabinet a Cabinet?" *Mississippi Valley Historical Review,* Vol. XLIV, no. I (June 1957), pp. 94-108.

Lowell, Edward J. *The Hessians and Other German Auxiliaries of Great Britain in the Revolutionary War.* New York: Harper & Brothers, 1884.

Lynch, Denis Tilden. *An Epoch and a Man: Martin Van Buren and His Times.* New York: Horace Liveright, 1929.

McCarthy, Charles. "The Antimasonic Party." *Annual Report of the American Historical Association,* Vol. 1 (1902), pp. 367-574.

McCormick, Richard P. *The Second American Party System: Party Formation in the Jacksonian Era.* Chapel Hill, N.C.: University of North Carolina Press, 1966.

MacDonald, William. "The Jackson and Van Buren Papers." *Proceedings of the American Antiquarian Society.* New Series, Vol. 17 (Worcester, Mass., 1970), pp. 231-38.

McFaul, John M. *See* Gatell, Frank Otto.

McGrane, Reginald Charles. *The Panic of 1837: Some Financial Problems of the Jacksonian Era.* New York: Russell & Russell, 1965.

McLemore, Richard Aubrey. *Franco-American Diplomatic Relations, 1816–1836.* University, La.: Louisiana State University Press, 1941.

Macleod, Henry Dunning. *The Theory and Practice of Banking.* 2 vols. London: Longmans, Green, Reader, and Dyer, 1879.

McMaster, John Bach. *A History of the People of the United States, from the Revolution to the Civil War.* 8 vols. New York: D. Appleton and Company, 1914.

Marshall, Lynn L. "The Authorship of Jackson's Bank Veto Message." *Mississippi Valley Historical Review,* Vol. L, no. 3 (December 1963), pp. 466–77.

Martineau, Harriet. *Society in America.* 2 vols. New York and London: Saunders & Otley, 1837.

Mayo, Bernard. *Henry Clay: Spokesman of the New West.* Boston: Houghton Mifflin Company, 1937.

Meigs, William M. *The Life of John Caldwell Calhoun.* 2 vols. New York: G. E. Stechert & Co., 1917.

Merriam, Charles Edward, and Gosnell, Harold Foote. *The American Party System: An Introduction to the Study of Political Parties in the United States.* New York: The Macmillan Company, 1949.

Meyers, Marvin. *The Jacksonian Persuasion: Politics and Belief.* Stanford, Calif.: Stanford University Press, 1957.

Morison, Samuel Eliot. *Harrison Gray Otis, 1765–1848: The Urbane Federalist.* Boston: Houghton Mifflin Company, 1969.

Nevins, Allan. *See* Hone, Philip.

Nichols, Roy F. *The Invention of the American Political Parties.* New York: The Macmillan Company, 1967.

Ogg, Frederic Austin. *The Reign of Andrew Jackson.* Philadelphia: J. B. Lippincott Company, 1963.

Parish, John Carl. *The Emergence of the Idea of Manifest Destiny.* Los Angeles: University of California Press, 1932.

Parton, James. *Life of Andrew Jackson.* 3 vols. New York: Mason Brothers, 1861.

BIBLIOGRAPHY

Pearce, Roy Harvey. *The Savages of America: A Study of the Indian and the Idea of Civilization.* Baltimore: The Johns Hopkins Press, 1953.

Pessen, Edward. *Jacksonian America: Society, Personality, and Politics.* Homewood, Ill.: The Dorsey Press, 1969.

_____. *Most Uncommon Jacksonians: The Radical Leaders of the Early Labor Movements.* Albany: State University of New York Press, 1967.

Poage, George Rawlings. *Henry Clay and the Whig Party.* Chapel Hill, N.C.: University of North Carolina Press, 1936.

Pollack, Queena. *Peggy Eaton, Democracy's Mistress.* New York: Milton, Balch and Company, 1931.

Remini, Robert V., *Andrew Jackson.* New York: Twayne Publishers, 1966.

_____. *The Election of Andrew Jackson.* Philadelphia: J. B. Lippincott Company, 1963.

_____. *Martin Van Buren and the Making of the Democratic Party.* New York: Columbia University Press, 1959.

_____, ed. *The Age of Jackson.* Columbia, S.C.: University of South Carolina Press, 1972.

Rezneck, Samuel. "The Depression of 1819-1822, a Social History." *American Historical Review,* Vol. XXXIX, no. 1, pp. 28-47.

Rogin, Michael Paul. *Fathers and Children: Andrew Jackson and the Subjugation of the American Indian.* New York: Alfred A. Knopf, 1975.

Roosevelt, Theodore. *Thomas Hart Benton.* New York: Charles Scribner's Sons, 1926.

Rozwene, Edwin C., ed. *Ideology and Power in the Age of Jackson.* New York: New York University Press, 1964.

Schlesinger, Arthur M., Jr. *The Age of Jackson.* Boston: Little, Brown and Company, 1945.

Schurz, Carl. *Life of Henry Clay.* 2 vols. Boston: Houghton Mifflin Company, 1887.

Sellers, Charles Grier, Jr. *James K. Polk, Jacksonian, 1795-1843.* Princeton, N.J.: Princeton University Press, 1957.

_____, ed. *Andrew Jackson, Nullification, and the State-Rights Tradition.* Chicago: Rand McNally & Company, 1963.

_____. "Andrew Jackson Versus the Historians." *Mississippi Valley Historical Review,* Vol. XLIV, no. 4 (March 1958), pp. 615-34.

————. "Jackson Men with Feet of Clay." *American Historical Review*, Vol. LXII, no. 3 (April 1957), pp. 537–51.

Sharp, James Roger. *The Jacksonians Versus the Banks: Politics in the States after the Panic of 1837.* New York: Columbia University Press, 1970.

Sharpe, Philip B. *The Rifle in America.* New York: Funk & Wagnalls Company, 1958.

Shepard, Edward M. *Martin Van Buren.* Boston: Houghton Mifflin and Company, 1890.

Singleton, Esther. *The Story of the White House.* 2 vols. New York: The McClure Company, 1907.

Slotkin, Richard. *Regeneration Through Violence: The Mythology of the American Frontier, 1600–1860.* Middletown, Conn.: Wesleyan University Press, 1973.

Smith, Margaret Bayard. *The First Forty Years of Washington Society*, Gaillard Hunt, ed. New York: Charles Scribner's Sons, 1906.

Smith, Walter Buckingham. *Economic Aspects of the Second Bank of the United States.* Cambridge, Mass.: Harvard University Press, 1953.

Stanwood, Edward. *A History of the Presidency from 1788 to 1897.* Boston: Houghton Mifflin Company, 1898.

Sumner, Charles Graham. *Protectionism.* New York: Henry Holt and Company, 1885.

Sumner, William Graham. *Andrew Jackson.* Boston: Houghton Mifflin Company, 1910.

Syrett, Harold C. *Andrew Jackson: His Contribution to the American Tradition.* Indianapolis: The Bobbs-Merrill Company, 1953.

Taussig, F. W. *The Tariff History of the United States.* New York: G. P. Putnam's Sons, 1914.

Temin, Peter. *The Jacksonian Economy.* New York: W. W. Norton & Company, 1969.

Tocqueville, Alexis de. *Democracy in America.* 2 vols. New York: Alfred A. Knopf, 1954.

Trollope, Mrs. *Domestic Manners of the Americans.* Barre, Mass.: Imprint Society, 1969.

Turner, Frederick Jackson. *Rise of the New West.* New York: Harper & Brothers Publishers, 1906.

BIBLIOGRAPHY

_____. *The United States, 1830-1850: The Nation and Its Sections.* New York: Henry Holt and Company, 1935.

Tyler, Alice Felt. *Freedom's Ferment: Phases of American Social History to 1860.* Minneapolis: University of Minnesota Press, 1944.

Van Buren, Martin. *Autobiography,* John C. Fitzpatrick, ed. New York: Augustus M. Kelley, 1969.

Van Deusen, Glyndon G. *The Jacksonian Era, 1828-1848.* New York: Harper and Row, Publishers, 1959.

_____. *Thurlow Weed: Wizard of the Lobby.* New York: DeCapo Press, 1969.

Von Holst, H. *John C. Calhoun.* Boston: Houghton Mifflin Company, 1899.

Ward, John William. *Andrew Jackson, Symbol for an Age.* New York: Oxford University Press, 1955.

Weed, Thurlow. *The Life of Thurlow Weed.* Boston: Houghton Mifflin, 1883.

Wellman, Paul I. *The House Divides: The Age of Jackson and Lincoln, from the War of 1812 to the Civil War.* Garden City, N.Y.: Doubleday & Company, 1966.

White, Leonard D. *The Federalists: A Study in Administrative History.* New York: The Macmillan Company, 1948.

_____. *The Jacksonians: A Study in Administrative History, 1829-1861.* New York: The Macmillan Company, 1954.

_____. *The Jeffersonians: A Study in Administrative History, 1801-1829.* New York: The Macmillan Company, 1951.

Wilburn, Jean Alexander. *Biddle's Bank: The Crucial Years.* New York: Columbia University Press, 1967.

Young, Mary E. "The Creek Frauds: A Study in Conscience and Corruption." *Mississippi Valley Historical Review,* Vol. XLII, no. 3 (December 1955), pp. 411-37.

_____. "Indian Removal and Land Allotment: The Civilized Tribes and Jacksonian Justice." *American Historical Review,* Vol. LXIV, no. 1, (October 1958), pp. 31-45.

INDEX

INDEX

INDEX

www.ingramcontent.com/pod-product-compliance
Lightning Source LLC
Chambersburg PA
CBHW021226090426
42740CB00006B/405